IMAGES
of Rail

Virginia & Truckee Railroad

Railroad to the Comstock

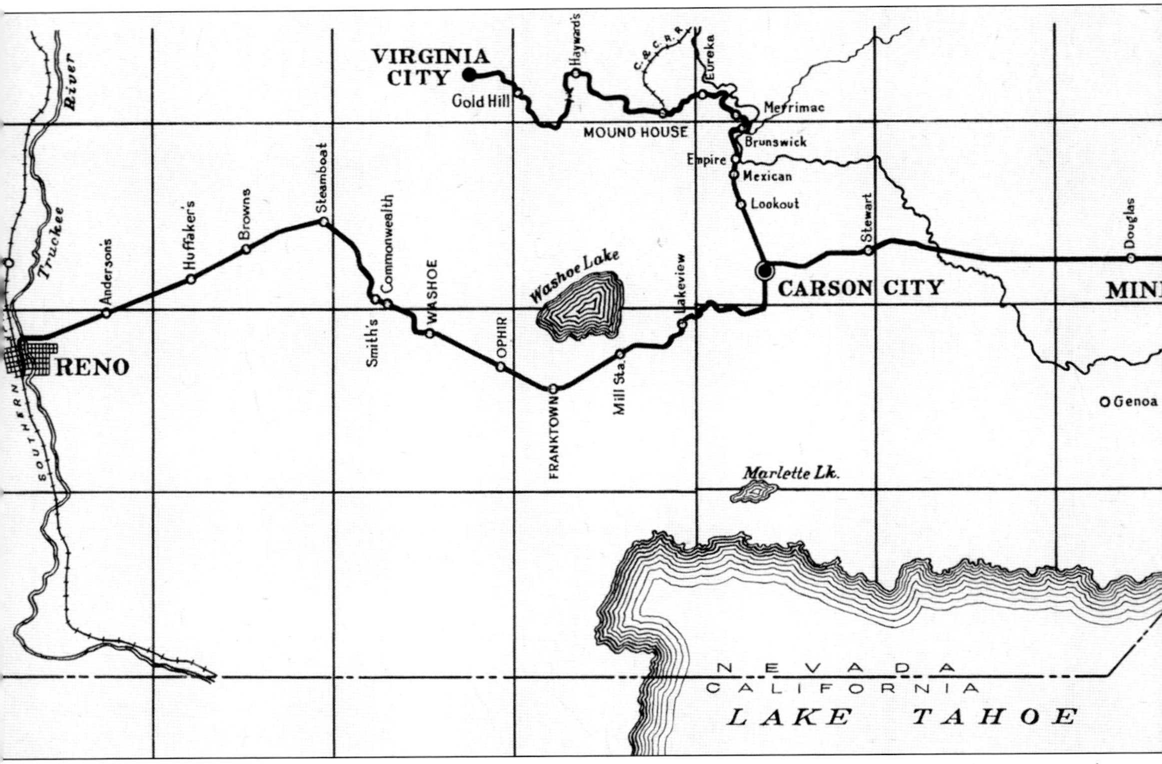

Virginia & Truckee Railroad: Railroad to the Comstock is a pictorial travel guide to Nevada's historic shortline railroad. It follows the geographic route, the communities, and the facilities of the completed 67-mile railroad from Reno to Virginia City and from Carson City down to Minden. Architect Frederic J. Shaw's map was drawn for a 1946 commemorative wall calendar of the Railroadians of America. (Frederic J. Shaw collection, California State Railroad Museum.)

ON THE COVER: Nevada governor Richard Kirman Sr. poses alongside the venerable 1872 Virginia & Truckee (V&T) locomotive No. 11 *Reno* on June 5, 1938, in the V&T's Carson City Yards. A native of Virginia City and former mayor of Reno, Kirman knew the V&T well and was only too happy to welcome the 200 railroad enthusiasts who gathered for one last trip by rail to the Comstock. (Gilbert H. Kneiss collection.)

IMAGES
of Rail

Virginia & Truckee Railroad

Railroad to the Comstock

Stephen E. Drew

ARCADIA
PUBLISHING

ISBN 978-1-4671-0741-9

Published by Arcadia Publishing
Charleston, South Carolina

Printed in the United States of America

Library of Congress Control Number: 2021945982

For all general information, please contact Arcadia Publishing:
Telephone 843-853-2070
Fax 843-853-0044
E-mail sales@arcadiapublishing.com
For customer service and orders:
Toll-Free 1-888-313-2665

Visit us on the Internet at www.arcadiapublishing.com

To Anya, Abigail, and Ivy, so you will know what grandpa has been working on.

Contents

ACKNOWLEDGMENTS

Researching the Virginia & Truckee Railroad has been a labor of love for more than five decades. Several institutions have generously made available their extensive holdings of original V&T materials including the Bancroft Library at UC Berkeley, the California State Railroad Museum in Sacramento, the Henry E. Huntington Library and Art Gallery in San Marino, the Nevada Historical Society in Reno, the Nevada State Railroad Museum in Carson City, and Special Collections at the University of Nevada–Reno Library.

Fellow V&T researchers and enthusiasts have been gracious in freely sharing the results of their research and insights, including Donald L. Ball, Michael A. Collins, Dale B. Darney, Richard C. Datin Jr., Christopher C. de Witt, Thomas H. Gray, Wendell W. Huffman, Cliff A. Jennings, Kent Kristiansson, Paul S. Martineau, Curtis A. Reid, Charles D. Siebenthal, Thomas B. Smith, and Kyle K. Wyatt.

Several acknowledged institutions, private collectors, and families of former V&T employees similarly made images available. This project was also an opportunity to draw from the breadth of photographic work from 1935 through 1950 by longtime colleague Ted G. Wurm, whose uncle James T. Savage was a V&T trainman for more than 40 years. The acknowledgment NSRM indicates images generously made available by the Nevada State Railroad Museum in Carson City. Similarly, CSRM indicates images from the California State Railroad Museum in Sacramento.

Unless otherwise noted, all other pictures and historical documents are from the collection of the author.

Finally, I am indebted to Beverly, my best friend and amazing wife of nearly 50 years, without whom this work would not have been possible.

The research continues.

INTRODUCTION

The story of the Virginia & Truckee Railroad mirrors the history of the Nevada Comstock Lode. Born of necessity to transport wood and ore products, the V&T was in place to enjoy the peak production and fabulous wealth of the 1873–1878 Big Bonanza. Afterward, it hung on through a gradual decline, with occasional bursts of renewed activity, until the last train ran in 1950—on the eve of the Comstock's new bonanza in tourism. Today, the V&T lives again with public steam train rides to and from the Comstock and restored equipment preserved at state railroad museums in Nevada, California, and Pennsylvania.

The V&T was created on March 5, 1868, by principals in the Bank of California to provide dependable transportation for the bank's portfolios of Comstock mines and mills. Leading the effort were shrewd Virginia City bank manager William Sharon, bank cashier William C. Ralston, and president Darius Ogden Mills down in San Francisco. Merrimac Mill superintendent Henry Marvin Yerington was recruited in 1869 to be the railroad's on-site superintendent. Using $500,000 in bonds issued by Storey and Ormsby Counties, $735,000 advanced by local mining companies, plus stock purchases and private loans, the V&T completed 21 miles of track between Carson City and Virginia City in January 1870; a 31-mile extension between Reno and Carson City opened effective October 1, 1872. Well-appointed passenger service promptly connected with the transcontinental railroad of the Central Pacific—later Southern Pacific—at Reno. The railroad's route was a feat of civil engineering championed by Isaac E. James who established the circuitous route while keeping the ruling grade to no more than 2.2 percent from Carson City up to Virginia City.

At its peak, the V&T owned 24 well-maintained steam locomotives, 18 attractive passenger cars, and several hundred very functional freight cars. It had a significant physical plant, a dozen stations, well-appointed shop facilities, and several hundred employees; ran up to 50 trains per day; paid dividends of up to $130,000 per month for its handful of stockholders; and was a significant political force to be reckoned with. The success spawned investments by the principals in affiliated mines, mills, lumber, water, mineral, newspaper, and other railroad ventures throughout western Nevada and eastern California. At one point, Yerington was president of at least 16 different companies headquartered out of his office in the V&T depot at Carson City.

Forest products were an essential element and one of the profitable side businesses. Large timbers were needed in the underground mines, lumber was essential for building, and everyone needed cordwood to burn as fuel for heat, cooking, and in the boilers of hoisting and pumping machinery. Wood products cut at Lake Tahoe were barged to sawmills at Glenbrook, hauled by narrow gauge train to Spooner Summit, flumed to Carson City, and then hauled by the V&T to the Comstock. On the return, the trains brought down ore from the mines to the mills; the principal investors were all part of the Bank of California crowd. It was a well-oiled machine with many common investors and directors. The spin-offs were numerous, with great optimism in Nevada and its continued mineral wealth.

But with every boom comes an inevitable bust. Operations during the 1890s depression years were particularly frugal. A new turn-of-the-century ore bonanza at Tonopah ushered in a new brief era of prosperity during which the V&T purchased additional equipment, replaced rails, and built a 15-mile extension south from Carson City in 1906 to tap developing ranch and agricultural interests in Minden and the Carson Valley. Reorganization occurred in 1905 as the V&T Railroad became the new V&T Railway.

V&T president D.O. Mills died in January 1910 and was succeeded by his son Ogden Mills in New York. Henry Yerington was at the local helm of the V&T for 40 years until he died in November 1910. The succeeding on-site managers consisted of Alexander M. Ardery, Herbert H. Coffin, Franklin E. Murphy, Samuel C. Bigelow, and finally, Gordon A. Sampson through 1950. Organized in 1864, the once all-powerful Bank of California quietly went out of existence in its 132nd year.

Competition from rubber-tired vehicles increasingly made inroads on the railroad's freight and passenger traffic. The railway's first red ink operations coincided with the completion of the 16-foot-wide concrete highway between Reno and Carson City in 1924. In 1933, the Mills Estate bought out the remaining one-third interest in the V&T held by the Sharon and Yerington interests and became sole owner of the railway. D.O. Mills's grandson Ogden Livingston Mills backed lines of credit to keep the V&T running during the increasingly lean years. His death in October 1937 led V&T management to seek voluntary federal receivership from April 1938 through January 1946.

Hollywood discovered the V&T in 1937 with some location filming and subsequent purchases of several dozen locomotives and cars over the next decade. Service to Virginia City was suspended in mid-1938 and the rails from Carson City to the Comstock were pulled up in late 1941. Sales of capital assets—rails and equipment—were used to support the day-to-day operations of the railway. In the end, there were only two dozen employees left, several of whom had been with the V&T for 30 to 40 years.

The end came on May 31, 1950, with the last scheduled train between Reno and Minden. The V&T concluded 80 years of continuous operations. Disposing of the remaining property and winding up the railway's financial affairs consumed another 13 years until the final dissolution occurred on December 13, 1963.

The V&T lay fallow until the late Robert C. Gray and his family brought the railroad back into operation out of Virginia City beginning on July 2, 1976. Seasonal V&T passenger operations now continue from May through October and during holidays.

This book details the history of the V&T and photographically follows the geographical route of the railroad, illuminating its facilities and the communities it served. It comes at an opportune time, during the sesquicentennial of the V&T's first service between Reno to Virginia City.

It is an engaging story of an amazing railroad. All aboard!

One

Reno

Gateway to the V&T

Reno was the gateway to the Virginia & Truckee Railroad.

The Central Pacific (CP) was building east into Nevada in May 1868 when it selected the name of Army general Jesse Lee Reno for what had been Lake's Crossing—Myron C. Lake's toll bridge across the Truckee River. The new town grew up around the railroad. The population was just over 1,000 when the Virginia & Truckee connected at Reno with the transcontinental rails of the Central Pacific—later the Southern Pacific—in July 1871.

Early Reno was a tough and, at times, seedy town that was overshadowed by nearby Virginia City and the Comstock Lode. V&T general superintendent Henry M. Yerington disdained setting foot in Reno. When transferring between the trains of the V&T and the CP, he chose instead to quietly wait until the last moment aboard the security of the passenger cars.

For nearly 80 years, a V&T passenger train departed Reno each morning for the three-hour trip to the end of the line. After a midday layover, the returning train reached Reno in the evening or late afternoon. The V&T's schedule was set to make close connections with trains on the CP's overland line.

From 1876 to 1881, busy travelers used the overnight Lightning Express train to make the 17.5-hour trip from San Francisco to Virginia City. Heading east, dinner was on the boat from San Francisco and breakfast was available at Carson City. The schedule allowed a full day for transacting business on the Comstock. The returning through train left Virginia City at 7:00 p.m., reaching San Francisco at 11:10 a.m. the next morning. Sleeping accommodations were available in the Central Pacific's Silver Palace Sleepers between Carson City and San Francisco.

Reno survived devastating fires in 1873 and 1879, rebuilding after each one. The town captured the University of Nevada in 1886, and in 1910, the population finally passed 10,000 inhabitants.

The V&T's last train into Reno was on May 31, 1950, forever severing a daily transcontinental connection that had been in place for nearly 80 years.

An eastbound Central Pacific passenger train stops at the first Reno station in this August 1868 stereo view taken from the platform of the freight warehouses on the opposite side of the tracks. The CP station was a depot hotel operated by William R. Chamberlain. A full third story and cupola were added before the building was lost in the Great Reno Fire of March 1879. (Photograph by Alfred A. Hart.)

Reno's new 47-room depot hotel opened in July 1879. The 32-by-170-foot structure cost $25,000 and fronted on the CP's tracks in Reno. On the back or south side was the V&T's single track from Carson City. Robert Perry and J. Fitzgerald succeeded Chamberlain as operators of the CP hotel in January 1886. Unfortunately, the grand depot burned to the ground on May 26, 1889. (California Historical Society.)

V&T locomotive No. 11 is ready for its early-morning departure from Reno around 1910. After two wooden depots, the CP's third Reno passenger station was a one-story structure built of bricks. High-quality, privately-owned hotels obviated the earlier railroad-subsidized public houses. Reno's population was just over 5,000 when the new 32-by-159-foot brick depot opened in 1889. (Photograph by Stanley G. Palmer.)

Reno's fourth overland depot was built for Southern Pacific (SP) by general contractors Ryberg & Sorenson of Salt Lake City, Utah. The completed 35-by-254-foot Mediterranean Revival structure was dedicated on February 8, 1926. From 1926 to 1950, the V&T paid SP to handle its station needs in Reno. Now used by Amtrak, the depot is one of the oldest buildings in the downtown area.

The V&T's track connection with the CP/SP at Reno took off just before the depot and ran along the back of the structure before heading across the Truckee River. Just south and across the street from the depot was Commercial Row, the heart of the city's first business center, which eventually became "gambler's row."

The V&T's track in the foreground curves into Commercial Row and around the depot. For many years, the Palace Hotel and Saloon on Commercial Row at Center Street was the largest gambling house in the state. Nevada did not outlaw gambling until 1910. (Nevada Historical Society.)

V&T locomotive No. 18, named *Dayton*, pulls a special passenger train across Commercial Row around 1908 on the westernmost interchange track between the V&T and the main line tracks of the Southern Pacific through Reno. Extra excursion trains transported passengers to local agricultural fairs, picnics, prize fights, patriotic parades, and other special events along the V&T. (Photograph by William E. Cann.)

This 1922 aerial view looks southeast across the Reno passenger station. A heavyweight passenger car is on the V&T's west-side interchange track while the McKeen Motor Car, the Riverside Mill, and the V&T-SP freight interchange yard are visible to the east of the depot—just past the elevated watchtower at Lake Street. (Nevada Historical Society.)

V&T locomotive No. 12 *Genoa* has backed the four-car morning passenger train up to the Reno depot. No. 12's tender is fully loaded with 2,200 gallons of water and three cords of wood, ready for the 52-mile trip to Virginia City. The *Genoa* is resplendent in the morning sunshine, fresh out of the V&T shop after an extensive October 1901 to April 1902 rebuild. (Gilbert H. Kneiss collection.)

Locomotive No. 11 *Reno* was the crew's favorite engine for handling the daily Virginia Express passenger train out of Reno. Behind No. 11, the smoke drifting above the express car's stove around 1910 indicates that the Wells, Fargo & Company express car is occupied and being loaded in preparation for the morning trip to Virginia City. (Photograph by Stanley G. Palmer.)

It is late afternoon by the time locomotive No. 26 and its two passenger cars arrive back at the Reno depot after their daylong, 92-mile round trip to Minden. Behind the 4-6-0 are the SP depot baggage room, the waiting room, offices, the Railway Express Agency building, and SP's concrete freight depot. (Photograph by Stuart A. Liebman.)

It is May 27, 1950, the final week of the V&T's operations. The depot train board lists a dozen arrivals and departures of SP passenger trains at Reno. The morning departure and evening arrival of the V&T's sole mixed passenger and freight train is listed at the bottom of the large board. Within a week, 80 years of V&T operations would come to a close. (Photograph by Kenneth W. Yeo.)

In the early years of the V&T, Reno generated cattle for the California market. But soon, most loaded freight cars simply rolled through town, from the CP onto the V&T, to meet the growing needs of the Comstock. The Riverside Mill Company was an exception with its origins in 1872 on East Second Street. Served by the V&T, the roller flour mill was one of the state's largest manufacturing concerns. (Photograph by Stanley G. Palmer, NSRM.)

The Riverside Mill's turn-of-the-century soda cracker plant was repurposed for warehousing by 1942 when No. 26 crept past, toward the Reno station. On the left, the two spur tracks were connected on the east end by 1936 as designated freight interchange tracks between the V&T and SP. The Riverside Mill buildings survived repeated fires until they were finally razed in the mid-1980s. (Photograph by James F. Orem.)

For about 20 years beginning in 1886, the water-powered Reno Reduction Works did custom ore processing on the north bank of the Truckee River—about a mile east of Reno. During July–September 1889, the V&T's first locomotive—the 1869 *Lyon*—was used temporarily in stationary boiler service at the works. The *Lyon* was dismantled a decade later. (Photograph by Charles H. Peters, CSRM.)

The Nevada Engineering Works was opposite the Riverside Mill on the north side of the SP main line. Organized in 1902, the substantial works were a major supplier of mining machinery, boilers, ore cars, and engineering equipment during more than two decades for the Comstock, Tonopah, Goldfield, and eastern Nevada. (Grahame H. Hardy collection.)

The V&T's 142-foot-long Howe-truss bridge across the Truckee River was completed in September 1871 by contractor Amasa Thompson, an early resident of Reno. The single-track bridge carried the main line of the V&T for 23 years before it was replaced by a steel structure. This view looks upstream toward Reno and the Sierra Nevada. (Roy D. Graves collection.)

The early-morning Virginia Express heads south across the Truckee River bridge in 1906. In tow is the four-car winter passenger train of express No. 14, mail and baggage No. 13, smoker No. 3, and coach No. 18. The woodburning 4-4-0 is about to pass the V&T's 8,568-gallon insulated water tank at Reno. (Photograph by Stanley G. Palmer.)

In early 1905, the V&T prepared for a new and larger turntable for turning engines at Reno. The old 50-foot A-frame turntable was jacked and cribbed out, the back of the engine house was taken down to shorten it from two to a single locomotive, and the shed was moved east to make more room for the new turntable. (Photograph by Stanley G. Palmer, NSRM.)

Early on the morning of March 20, 1949, No. 26 was run out onto the Reno turntable in preparation for handling the day's sole passenger train. The 57-foot-long riveted turntable was purchased secondhand for $2,090 in early 1905 from the Walter A. Zelnicker Supply Company of St. Louis. The 75-ton capacity turntable ably served the V&T through the end of operations in 1950. (Photograph by Robert C. Gray.)

The V&T is on the left in this June 1911 view looking west down the main line of Southern Pacific through Reno. The railroad was the backbone of Reno. The Central Pacific arrived in June 1868 and was leased to Southern Pacific beginning in 1885. The CP merged into SP in 1959 and SP was sold to Union Pacific in 1996, with continued daily operations through Reno. (Marvin T. Maynard collection.)

Reno also had narrow gauge railroads beginning in 1880. Begun as the Nevada & Oregon, it would become the Nevada-California-Oregon (NCO) in 1893. The NCO's early steam locomotives were all repaired by the V&T shops in Carson City. The NCO extended 236 miles from Reno to Lakeview, Oregon, in 1912. The 64-mile Reno-Herlong track was sold in 1917 to Western Pacific. The remaining trackage was sold to Southern Pacific in 1926.

Reno had other railroads as well. Reno Traction streetcars occupy Second Street in this c. 1910 view looking east from Sierra Street. The fare between Reno and Sparks was 10¢. Nevada Transit, Reno Traction, and Nevada Interurban operated nearly 11 miles of track for more than 20 years. The last car ran in September 1927. (Photograph by William E. Cann.)

The V&T's 1873 wood-burning *Genoa* and combination car No. 16 operated on May 9, 1953, for three miles on the Western Pacific out of Reno. The occasion was a National Model Railroad Association excursion. The locomotive had returned west after operating at the 1948–1949 Chicago Railroad Fair. (Western Pacific Railroad.)

The train has just pulled out of the depot and the view from the cupola of V&T caboose-coach No. 24 confirms that Commercial Row is still a busy place in "the Biggest Little City in the World." The city's population in the late 1940s exceeded 30,000, and gambling and tourism were the largest industries. Below, a Southern Pacific ALCO PA struts across Virginia Street pulling the eastbound Overland. Resplendent in SP's distinctive Daylight paint scheme, the 1946–1953 units epitomized the modern diesel-electric motive power that helped usher in the demise of the steam-powered V&T. (Above, Grahame H. Hardy collection; below, Southern Pacific Railroad.)

Two

Washoe Valley

Farms and Flumes

Heading south from Reno, the Virginia & Truckee traversed the Truckee Meadows, Pleasant Valley, the expansive Washoe Valley, Eagle Valley, and finally into Carson City, a distance of 31 miles by rail from Reno.

The Truckee Meadows south of Reno was originally a sparse region of sagebrush and native grasses. Beginning in the 1860s, local farmers organized some 40 ditch companies to deliver Truckee River water to farms and ranches as far south as Washoe Valley. Paralleling early stage routes, the V&T's first stations south of Reno were small communities and stage stops consisting of William Anderson's large hay ranch, Granville W. Huffaker's farm, and Peleg "Felix" Brown's farm and ranch.

Eleven miles south of Reno were the natural mineral hot springs dubbed Steamboat Springs, which had a hotel and seasonal resort. Immediately south was Smiths—the extensive Pleasant Valley ranch of George S. Smith. Further south was Galena, an early lumber camp and later a mining district.

Midway on the Reno to Carson City line was Washoe Canyon opening into Washoe City at the north end of Little Washoe Lake. The first seat of Washoe County, Washoe City was the terminus for the large wood flume operated by Pete N. Marker and C. Bastin.

Heading down along the west side of Washoe Lake, the V&T passed through the stock and racehorse ranch of Theodore Winters, the early milling town of Ophir, and past the famous Bowers Mansion of "Sandy" and Eilley Orum Bowers—the Comstock's first millionaires.

After the agricultural community of Franktown and the lumber yard at Mill Station, the railroad crested the divide between Washoe and Eagle Valleys at Lakeview, which was aptly named for its overview of nearby Washoe Lake.

From Lakeview, it was all downhill into Eagle Valley and Nevada's capital city. The 31-mile trip usually took 80 minutes, with minimal curvature, and a net change in elevation of just over 200 feet. It was a magnificent ride.

Stanley G. Palmer was an undergraduate student at the University of Nevada, Reno when he took these V&T photographs just south of Reno around 1906. With a faster shutter, doing his own darkroom work, and pushing the speed of the film, Palmer was able to capture remarkable early morning action shots of the V&T before he headed off to class. Above, with cylinder cocks wide open, new coal-burning Second No. 25 heads south with the Virginia Express. On the right are Long Siding, the Western Union Telegraph line, and a low stone fence marking the east side of the railroad's 40-foot-wide right-of-way and what would eventually become Holcomb Avenue. Below, the 1875 wood-burning *Inyo* is on the point of the four-car passenger train as it heads south toward Washoe Valley. (Both photographs by Stanley G. Palmer.)

The V&T's afternoon local was a mixed train of both passenger and freight cars. Photographer Palmer stands on the platform of the combination car, looking south toward Huffaker Hills and an impressive string of loaded freight cars. From 1875 to 1880, Huffakers was the terminus of the 15-mile Pacific Wood, Lumber & Flume Company "V" flume controlled by John W. Mackay and James G. Fair. (Photograph by Stanley G. Palmer, NSRM.)

The fireman leans broadly out the left-side cab of new coal-burning Second No. 25, a 1905 product of the Baldwin Locomotive Works of Philadelphia. The 4-6-0 was purchased primarily for hauling 50-ton ore cars from Mound House to Virginia City and for the new lumber traffic from Truckee. In tow today are six passenger cars for the morning Virginia Express to Virginia City. (Photograph by Stanley G. Palmer.)

The heart of Browns was a 620-acre farm, ranch, and early stage station begun in 1858 by Peleg "Felix" Brown. The main house was built in 1864 and still stands. The V&T main line was behind the home and outbuildings. A V&T sidetrack was used by Brown and other local farmers to load hay cars for the Comstock. (Damonte family, Historic American Buildings Survey)

The open end door of caboose-coach No. 24 frames an April 1950 view looking north through old Browns. Nine miles south of Reno, Browns was the terminus of the El Dorado Wood & Flume Company's six-mile "V" flume from Whites Canyon in the nearby Carson Range. Browns was a major wood station on the V&T from 1875 through 1883. (Photograph by Frank Wolf.)

"New" Browns was established with a new spur track after World War I for feed supply and cattle ranches operated by Frank E. Humphrey Jr., the Double Diamond Land & Live Stock Ranch, and H.M. "Rich" Richardson. Loaded stock cars of cattle at Browns still totaled 49 inbound loads and a dozen outbound carloads during 1948. Above, locomotive No. 26 leads the afternoon mixed train heading northbound through new Browns in 1948–1949. Below, photographers Brian and Audrey Thompson wave at the crew as locomotive No. 27 barrels south through new Browns on May 31, 1950. The V&T and the parallel two-lane highway were more than able to handle the usual light volume of traffic. (Above, photograph by A. Sheldon Pennoyer; below, photograph by Ted G. Wurm.)

This stereo view of Steamboat Springs Hotel was made around 1885 by Virginia City photographer John S. Noe. Looking northwest, the V&T main line from Carson City is on the left. The natural mineral hot springs were discovered in 1860 by Felix Monet. The springs were Nevada's first resort and therapeutic spa. The hotel was destroyed by fire in April 1901, and a replacement burned in June 1937. (Robert C. Dockery Collection, NSRM.)

Locomotive No. 26 heads a southbound nine-car mixed passenger and freight train into Steamboat around 1941. Behind stock cars and tank cars are mail and baggage Second No. 21 and passenger and express No. 20. Steamboat was considered a "flag stop," which meant that the conductor stopped the train only if there were passengers to be picked up or discharged. (Photograph by Ted Steinmetz.)

V&T management agreed for the final scheduled train to make a brief stop on May 31, 1950. The occasion was a short farewell by Steamboat area school children, coordinated by "the World's Smallest Chamber of Commerce." It was a touching ceremony of speeches, proclamations, farewells, and a tearful round of "Auld Lang Syne." During the V&T's 80 years of serving Steamboat, the community's official population rarely exceeded 25 inhabitants. The geothermal activity continues, but the V&T is but a memory. (Both photographs by Ted G. Wurm.)

The V&T shared the right-of-way with an early wagon road, later US Highway 395, at the entrance to Pleasant Valley. Settled by the Mormons in 1856, the small fertile valley was named for its pleasant aspects. Locomotive No. 26 steams north with its mixed train on August 11, 1946, a little over halfway on the 31-mile route between Carson City and Reno. (Photograph by Ted G. Wurm.)

Smiths derived its name from pioneer resident George S. Smith Sr., who settled in Pleasant Valley in 1858. This lithograph from Thompson and West's 1881 *History of Nevada* depicts a southbound V&T train skirting the back of the Smith Ranch. In the early 1900s, Smiths was a flag-stop for passengers. It also had a passing siding for opposing V&T trains.

This southbound mixed train has an assortment of at least 10 cars around 1906 as it climbs through Pleasant Valley. Bringing up the rear is one of the V&T's two identical combination passenger and baggage cars built by the Detroit Car Works in 1874. The two cars, V&T Nos. 15 and 16, are preserved at railroad museums in Nevada and California, respectively. (Photograph by Stanley G. Palmer, NSRM.)

The afternoon train has just picked up a loaded gondola car and is proceeding north past the Union Lead Mine in August 1946. South of Smiths, Galena or Commonwealth was the site of Parke's lumber mill in the 1870s and a series of lead, zinc, silver, gold, and copper mines during the early 1900s. (Photograph by Ted G. Wurm.)

V&T chief engineer Isaac E. James skillfully threaded the V&T right-of-way through Washoe or Allen's Canyon during his 1871 surveys. The railroad repeatedly crossed both a wagon road and Steamboat Creek on its route through the canyon. Local Native Americans had unique names for many of the distinctive rock formations. This image dates to October 1919. (Photograph by David J. Welch, NSRM.)

The V&T's last scheduled southbound train is dwarfed by the immense walls and echoes of Washoe Canyon. The fireman aboard locomotive No. 27 is accommodating photographers with lots of smoke. It is May 31, 1950, the end of 80 years of V&T service. (Photograph by Ted G. Wurm.)

Locomotive Second No. 5 crosses 72.5-foot-long trestle No. 17-E, the longest of the V&T's four stringer trestles through Washoe Canyon. Forty-year veteran Grover C. Russell is in the fireman's seat. It is Sunday, May 7, 1950, and No. 5 pulls a train of mail and baggage No. 23 plus passenger and express No. 18 for a chartered photographer's special. (Photograph by Alfred M. Rose Jr.)

Locomotive No. 27 heads across 47.5-foot-long trestle No. 17-F at the southern entrance to Washoe Canyon on May 31, 1950. Masonry blocks form the abutments for the six-stringer trestle over Steamboat Creek. The V&T's last scheduled train has cleared the US Highway 395 crossing at Washoe City and is en route north for its late afternoon arrival in Reno. (Photograph by Ted G. Wurm.)

Washoe City had a population of 2,500 and was the county seat of Washoe County from 1861 to 1871, at which time the courthouse was moved to Reno. The city had only several hundred inhabitants by the time the V&T arrived in 1872. During the 1870s, Washoe City was the terminus of Marker and Bastin's Washoe & White's Canyon Flume and the location of their large ice house. (Nevada Historical Society.)

Locomotive Second No. 5 heads south on what would have been F Street in Washoe City. The V&T maintained a depot office in the two-story structure at F and Second Streets during the 1870s and a telegraph office in the building through the 1890s. Of the three structures, only the single-story building at far right still stands. (Photograph by Alfred M. Rose Jr.)

The V&T's 70-foot-long McKeen Motor Car No. 22 rolls south through a deserted Washoe City around 1920. With added Railway Post Office and Railway Express Agency compartments, the innovative gasoline motorcar alternated daily service with the railway's steam train from 1933 through 1945. For 35 years, the "Big Red Devil" was a regular sight on the V&T. (Ellen Williams.)

The 1860s Carpenter's Gothic house, matching barn, and 6,000-acre ranch of Theodore "Thee" Winters was a little over a mile south of Washoe City. Winters was the first Nevadan to breed thoroughbreds for horseracing in the state. His standard-gauge private palace horse car was maintained by the V&T. Named *Nevada*, the car transported horses between Winters's ranches in Nevada and California and races around the United States. (Photograph by Joseph W. Johnson.)

Ophir was the site of the Ophir Silver Mining Company's $500,000 quartz mill from 1861–1873. Ore was hauled from Virginia City by wagon over Ophir Grade and a mile-long trestle across Washoe Lake. Beginning in 1875, William E. Price operated a cordwood ditch and flume, which terminated at Ophir. In 1899, Price sold the business to Samuel Longabaugh, who continued the operation for another decade. (Daun M. Bohall collection.)

A woman poses on the fence at a road crossing of the V&T near the Ophir icehouse track around 1900. William Price had two sawdust-insulated icehouses at Ophir during the 1880s and 1890s. Blocks of ice were sent down the flumes during winter months from his mountain lake reservoirs. Ice was in demand for both domestic purposes and in cooling rooms for Comstock miners. (Robert C. Dockery Collection, NSRM.)

The palatial Bowers Mansion home and grounds built by Lemuel Sanford "Sandy" Bowers and his wife, Eilley Orrum Bowers, were a popular destination on the V&T for picnics, music, dances, and swimming for more than 50 years. Women and children rode in V&T coaches while the men arrived on flatcars fitted with long benches. During special events, a couple of thousand revelers could be seen walking the last quarter-mile or so up Bowers Lane to the mansion and lush picnic grounds. (Right, photograph by Roy D. Graves; below, Yerington family collection.)

Franktown was laid out in 1856 by Mormon elder Orson Hyde. It boasted 500 inhabitants in 1864 and about half that by the time the V&T arrived in 1872. The V&T's 20-by-40-foot combination depot was the shipping hub for Washoe Valley, including produce and dairy products. The area also had good grazing pastures. The depot closed in February 1927 and was sold locally. (Nevada Historical Society.)

The V&T's last scheduled southbound train steams toward the railway's Franktown water tank on May 31, 1950. The 1901 replacement tank held 11,250 gallons and was in use through 1950. Opposite the tank is Emmy Wood's exclusive Flying ME dude-divorce ranch, a busy place when progressive Nevada divorce law required only six weeks of residency in the Sagebrush State. (Photograph by Ted G. Wurm.)

Mill Station was 2.5 miles below Franktown. The community of 300 was the first Washoe Valley logging and fluming depot serving the developing Comstock Lode. The V&T's 40-acre trackside lumber and wood yard moved in the late 1870s down to Lakeview. Beginning in the 1880s, the area was primarily farms and cattle ranches. Distinctive Slide Mountain looms behind Mill Station where the remaining V&T siding was retired in 1943.

This first-class ticket was stamped as sold on March 18, 1878, from Carson City to Mill Station. At the time, the one-way adult fare from Carson City to Virginia City was $2. Reno to Virginia City was $3. In comparison, a Comstock miner earned $4 per day working an eight-hour shift. A V&T engineer received $5 per day for working a 10-hour day, seven days a week. Travel by rail was not inexpensive.

Lakeview—originally Lake View—was the lumber yard of Walter S. Hobart and Seneca H. Marlette's Sierra Nevada Wood & Lumber Company (SNW&L). The operation involved an incline railway and flume between its sawmill at North Lake Tahoe and the waiting flatcars of the V&T at Lakeview. In mid-1880, its wood yard was shipping 400 cords of wood per day to the Comstock. (Nevada Historical Society.)

Mining timbers were discharged from the flume and then dragged down to the V&T. At its peak, SNW&L employed 250 men and owned thousands of acres of timberland adjacent to Lake Tahoe. Incorporated in April 1878, SNW&L concluded its Tahoe operations in October 1894 when its timber supply was exhausted. Three siphon lines of the Virginia & Gold Hill Water Company are in the background. (Nevada Historical Society.)

Locomotive No. 27 heads a southbound mixed train through Lakeview on September 6, 1948. Five miles north of Carson City, Lakeview had a passing siding and was home to the V&T's "Summit" section crew. Wheat was briefly shipped from Lakeview in 1912. In 1948, the population totaled five inhabitants. (Photograph by Wilbur C. Whittaker.)

No. 27 skirts the Lakeview Tunnel with a northbound mixed train in May 1937. The 367-foot-long tunnel bridged the divide between Washoe and Eagle Valleys. After six decades, the aging tunnel was prone to settling and repeated cave-ins at a time when freight cars were being made larger and heavier. In 1932, the railway hired Isbell Construction to build a new roadbed around the sagging tunnel. (Photograph by Gilbert H. Kneiss.)

The Lakeview grade was a formidable climb out of Carson City to the county line between Ormsby and Washoe Counties. The grade was punctuated with steep cuts and long fills. Heavy trains were often double-headed up the grade or were divided in half, with the engine making two trips before reassembling the consist for the rest of the trip north to Reno. (Robert C. Dockery Collection, NSRM.)

Locomotive No. 26 has just cleared Sand Cut, two miles out of Carson City. The nine-car mixed train is ready for its ascent on the Lakeview grade on July 9, 1938. At Sand Cut, sand was routinely shoveled onto flatcars for delivery along the railroad. After heavy braking coming down Lakeview grade, Sand Cut was the first scheduled eastbound stop before heading into Carson City. (Photograph by Ted G. Wurm.)

Three

Carson City
Nevada's Capital City

Carson City derives its name from John C. Fremont's trusted scout Christopher "Kit" Carson, who entered western Nevada during the winter of 1843–1844. Carson City has been the state capital since Nevada was admitted to the Union on October 31, 1864.

Groundbreaking for the V&T occurred at Carson City on February 18, 1869. The first rails extended east down Caroline Street from the new US Mint. The first three-track engine house, turntable, carpenter's shop, sand and coal house, and blacksmith shop were six blocks west. The original end-of-track was another mile west, up against the Carson Range at Ash Canyon, where the V&T had a water tank and a steady supply of cordwood for fuel. In late 1870, the railroad laid a one-mile spur track down Stewart Street to reach the Clear Creek wood flume coming through King's Canyon.

The impending 1872 completion of the V&T's 31-mile extension between Reno and Carson City was the impetus to build a 31-by-118-foot passenger depot adjacent to the Mint plus smaller depots at other stations along the line. A new main line passenger track was extended through town on Washington Street—one block north of the Caroline Street freight track.

A new 11-stall engine house and expansive shop buildings were developed beginning in 1873 in "northern" Carson City.

In 1896, the V&T's general office was transferred from Virginia City down to Carson City. Additional trackage from the depot in 1906 allowed a direct connection with the new 15-mile Minden Branch. In the 1920s, automobile dealerships and bulk petroleum products began generating additional carloads.

The V&T left Carson City for the last time on May 31, 1950. For many years, Carson City was the only state capital without any kind of railroad service.

Thirty years to the day after the last V&T train, the nucleus of the Nevada State Railroad Museum opened in Carson City with the largest and finest collection of V&T locomotives and cars extant.

A woman and two children walk the tracks of the V&T, approaching Carson City from the west. Printed in Germany, this early 20th-century 1¢ postcard was sold at Abe Cohn's well-known Emporium Basketry on North Carson Street in Carson City.

Carson City's population was just over 3,000 when a photographer climbed up to the cupola of the state capitol for three 1871 panoramas of the young city. In this view looking northwest toward the Carson Range, the V&T's original three-stall wooden engine house rises near the center on the west side of town. (Great Basin Gallery.)

The V&T's original three-track engine house was just off Caroline Street. Built as a 45-by-65-foot structure, it was quickly lengthened 55 feet on the west end to double its capacity. After the new 11-stall engine house was completed "downtown" in 1874, the structure became the car shed and "old roundhouse" for storing out-of-service locomotives and cars. (Photograph by David J. Welch.)

The new US Mint at Carson City is the large building in the center at North Carson and Caroline Streets in 1871. Across the street to the east sits a caboose and the V&T telegraph office. Immediately north, a site is being prepared along Washington Street for construction of the V&T's Carson City Passenger Depot. (Great Basin Gallery.)

A well-rehearsed bevy of daily activity is about to occur as locomotive No. 11 arrives at Carson City with the Virginia Express in June 1911. The four-car passenger train has a scheduled 15-minute stop to handle passengers and their baggage, US Mail, and Wells, Fargo & Company express before the conductor rings the station departure bell and shouts, "All aboard!" (Robert C. Dockery Collection, NSRM.)

Built in 1872 as a 118-foot-long structure, the depot was soon lengthened 26 feet on the east end for additional office space. For 78 years, the depot was also the general office for the V&T's senior on-site manager—initially Henry M. Yerington, followed by Alexander M. Ardery, Frank E. Murphy, Samuel C. Bigelow, and finally, Gordon A. Sampson. (Robert C. Dockery Collection, NSRM.)

The train crew gathers on the station platform alongside locomotive No. 26 and the daily eastbound mixed train on July 7, 1938. Two passenger cars—mail and baggage No. 13 and passenger and express No. 20—ably handle the traffic that only a few years earlier required four cars. The track in the foreground is for the gasoline motorcar operating to Virginia City. (Photograph by Albert C. Phelps.)

V&T vice president and general superintendent Henry Marvin Yerington is second from the right in this 1890s gathering of employees between the Carson depot offices of the master of transportation–train dispatcher and the general freight office. Yerington was a veritable institution at the V&T, holding the senior on-site management position from February 1869 until his death in November 1910. (Grahame H. Hardy collection.)

The 44-star American flag flies from the roof of the US Mint, where this photograph was taken in 1893 looking east down the main line of the V&T toward Empire City and the Carson River. On the lower right is the railroad's Carson City freight depot, which was moved down from Steamboat in 1872 and lengthened an additional 50 feet on the east end during the late 1880s. (Photograph by George D. Oliver.)

Locomotive Second No. 25 assembles the mixed passenger and freight train alongside the freight depot in Carson City in 1935. The scheduled departure time is 9:50 a.m. for Train No. 4 to Virginia City. The 4-6-0 often replaced usual daily motorcars Nos. 23 or 99 on Saturdays, when there were freight cars to be hauled up to Virginia City. The freight depot burned on December 31, 1962. (Photograph by David L. Joslyn.)

For 80 years, the V&T was a haven for stub switches. Stub switches had two moveable rails as opposed to tapered points or blades. The sideways action of the rails pushed snow to the side, instead of packing it between the points and the rail in more modern designs. This view into the Carson City yard on July 19, 1938, looks east over one of the V&T's unusual three-way stub switches.

Instead of a yard full of switches, a 54-foot-long turntable handled the responsibilities for the 11 tracks extending into the engine house and shops. The cast-iron turntable was purchased in 1873 for $2,250 from William Sellers & Company of Philadelphia and installed in a brick-lined pit. Tracks extended around two sides of the table by 1948, when it was spiked into a fixed position. (Photograph by William A. Pennington.)

The V&T's signature structure in Carson City was the mammoth 180-by-320-foot engine house and shops, custom-built of sandstone by prominent local builder Abram Curry. The stone edifice was the center building in a complex that eventually comprised over 40 structures. Posed outside for photographers on June 5, 1938, from left to right are locomotives Nos. 26 and 11, motorcar No. 99, and Second No. 25. (Photograph by William A. Pennington.)

The engine house was the overnight "garage" for steam locomotives. At its peak in June 1876, the V&T owned 24 steam locomotives and stabled them in rectangular engine houses and semi-circular roundhouses at Reno, Steamboat, Carson City, and Virginia City. On August 21, 1933, Verdi Lumber Company Shay No. 7 was also in the shop for repairs. (Photograph by David L. Joslyn.)

Local blacksmith Daniel L. Kelley was longtime foreman of the 57-by-60-foot blacksmith shop. The V&T shops not only took care of their own 400 locomotives and cars, but also performed repair work for the affiliated Carson & Colorado Railroad (C&C), as well as other railroads, mines, mills, and lumber companies within several hundred miles of Carson City. The V&T had a revered reputation for quality work. (Nevada State Museum.)

No. 26 was photographed in the back shop on July 14, 1937, for the last heavy repairs performed in the shops. The shops were gradually closed as shop foremen retired or died. As a consequence, major overhauls were deferred or were contracted out to the nearby Sparks, Nevada, shops of Southern Pacific. (Photograph by Ted G. Wurm.)

After the engine house, the next largest building in the shop complex was the 120-foot-long paint shop. Locomotives and cars received distinctive paint schemes in the early years and more standardized color schemes thereafter. In 60 years, from 1876 to 1936, the V&T only had two supervising master car and locomotive painters: David R. Culp and Joseph P. Castle. The shop closed when Castle died in 1936. (Photograph by David L. Joslyn.)

Another distinctive red building in the yard was the V&T's third Carson City water tank—an unusual double-spouted structure. The nearly rectangular insulated housing contains twin redwood tanks, each holding 6,000 gallons of water. On the left side in 1949 sits Lucius Beebe and Charles Clegg's private car *The Gold Coast* on the freight line. On the right is the through track from the passenger station. (Photograph by Roy D. Graves.)

This octagonal building along the south side of the shops is often confused with the water tank but it is the 26,000-gallon oil tank and adjoining sump, which were installed in 1907 when the V&T began converting its locomotives from burning cordwood and coal to fuel oil. With assistance from the fireman, Second No. 5 fills her tender during the V&T's final days. (William A. Pennington collection.)

The steel shell of the V&T's 1910 McKeen Motor Car No. 22 was sold locally in 1946 and became the popular Super Chief Diner in Carson City. The rare 70-foot-long car was acquired in 1996 by the Nevada State Railroad Museum and has since been meticulously restored to its operable c. 1910 appearance. (Photograph by Norman W. Holmes.)

The V&T's Clear Creek flume track extended south down Stewart Street for more than a mile to the vast lumber yard at the terminus of the 12-mile flume from Spooner's Summit. Logs cut around Lake Tahoe were towed by boat to the sawmills at Glenbrook, sawn into mining timbers and building lumber, and then floated down the flume to Carson City. Once in the valley, the main flume divided into three branches for wood storage over a wide area. Four V&T spur tracks extended along the sides of the discharging "V" flumes. The wood products were sorted by type, stacked, allowed to dry, and then loaded aboard V&T flatcars for the trip up the hill to Gold Hill and Virginia City. The underground mines of the Comstock became the final "tomb" for Sierra timbers. The daily transportation system continued through the 1898 cutting season. (Both photographs by Carleton E. Watkins.)

Nothing so rapidly changed the landscape than an overnight blanket of snow, particularly during the harsh winters of 1889–1890, 1915–1916, and 1937–1938. Above, the 1873 snow-plow locomotive No. 18 *Dayton* woods-up in the Carson City yard in 1889 before reassuming its position on the point of the eastbound passenger train to Virginia City. It would be a long, cold trip. To the right, a lone two-horse sleigh heads up Carson Street past the federal building and toward the US Mint and the V&T passenger depot. (Above, Nevada State Museum; right, Nevada Historical Society.)

Railroad enthusiasts discovered the V&T in 1938 and chartered nine railfan excursions over the road from 1938 through 1950. The Chicago Chapter of the Railway & Locomotive Historical Society poses aboard V&T flat car No. 6 on the depot platform at Carson City. In the background is Wells Fargo's two-story yellow "butter house" and a wood shed. For many of the Chicago excursionists, the V&T was the highlight of their 6,000-mile trek.

Five hundred passengers on the California-Nevada Railroad Historical Society's Farewell Excursion paused for lunch in the cavernous car shop at Carson City on May 29, 1949. The event was reminiscent of the grand railroad ball hosted in the same space by contractor Abram Curry on July 4, 1873, as the massive new stone engine house and shops were nearing completion. (Grahame H. Hardy collection.)

Four

Empire City

Quartz Reduction Mills

Heading east, the V&T had a passing siding at Lookout two miles outside of Carson City. One mile further, the railroad reached Empire City where it ran along the north bank of the Carson River. Originating in the Sierra Nevada, the river was important for farm irrigation, for use by huge seasonal wood drives of cordwood, and for powering the quartz reduction mills strung along the river from Empire City to Dayton.

Dams and ditches powered water wheels to operate the deafening stamps that crushed the ore. The flow of water in the Carson River varied seasonally with one or two months every year when the mills closed down due to low water. But the reliability and cost of free water outweighed other mills consuming cordwood and operating by steam power.

The Mexican and Morgan Mills were at Empire City, which often flooded during spring floods along the Carson River.

Next were the large Brunswick Mill and the short-lived Merrimac Mill, where the V&T's Henry M. Yerington was one of the early superintendents. The route of the V&T was circuitous as it wound along the side of the river and began its climb out of the canyon.

The main line was substantially above the Vivian and Santiago Mills as it continued its climb toward the Comstock. The last mill directly served by the V&T was the large Eureka Mill. The narrow-gauge Eureka Mill Railroad hauled its own small ore cars the final mile from the V&T ore dump down to the mill on the river.

Rising out of the Carson River Canyon toward the midway point of Mound House yielded the first view of Mt. Davidson—formerly Sun Mountain—in Virginia City. In the 10 miles from Carson City to Mound House, the ingenious route laid out by chief engineer "Ike" James provided fairly direct service to the major mills. Through the canyon, James successfully kept the curvature to 14 degrees or less on a continuous grade of no more than 90 feet to the mile. It was no small feat.

Established in 1861, the Mexican Mill was originally known as the Silver State Reduction Works. The mill dam was approximately 12 feet high and 100 feet wide, and had a fish ladder near its center, as seen in this 1889 image. Water entered the ditch at far right and was carried 4.5 miles to power 44 stamps. The V&T delivered ore via a long wooden trestle into the northeast end of the mill. (Yerington family collection.)

The Mexican Mill processed Comstock ore by traditional methods for 30 years until it was converted to a cyanide plant in 1891. This photograph dates to 1908 during the mill's final decade when it was repurposed for crushing gypsum from Mound House. The V&T's trackage was removed in 1909, and the mill was sold locally for junk the next year. (Robert C. Dockery Collection, NSRM.)

The V&T track is on the high ground on the right in this view looking west toward Empire City. The railroad skirted the northern edge of the community, which was prone to flooding by the Carson River. Early settlers humorously referred to Empire City as "the seaport town" due to spring floods. The Mexican Mill is the large structure on the west side of the river town. (Daun M. Bohall collection.)

Empire City lived up to its seaport nickname during the flood of March 1907, which inundated the city and washed out several mill dams. At far left is the V&T's combination freight and passenger depot. The railroad had similar though not identical 20-by-40-foot combination depots at Huffakers, Franktown, Empire City, and Mound House. (Photograph by Herman Davis, Nevada Historical Society.)

The Morgan Mill's earlier name, the Yellow Jacket Mill, is the title of this 1872 stereo view of the mill at Empire City. The V&T's main line passes through the center, with a single water tank on the north side and a raised passenger and freight platform on the south. The V&T soon added a second identical square-frame tank at Morgan and Scales when the number of thirsty steam locomotives increased.

The morning Virginia Express runs east past the Morgan Mill with one of the road's 4-4-0s pulling express No. 1, mail and baggage No. 2, and Brill coaches Nos. 11 and 12. The wood trestle supported a box flume that delivered water overhead from a nearby spring. The rows of cordwood fueled a 175-horsepower steam engine that allowed the mill to operate when water was low in the river. (Nevada Historical Society.)

The V&T main line is in the foreground while the railroad's 713-foot-long spur track into the Morgan Mill is on substantial wood bents for delivering and unloading the V&T's eight-ton bottom-dumping ore cars. In 1880, the mill employed nearly three dozen men. The facility utilized 40 stamps in 1890 for a crushing capacity of 110 tons per day. (Thomas B. Smith collection.)

Only the V&T platform remains alongside the Morgan Mill in 1908. The V&T's ore and wood spurs have been removed and the mill's machinery is in the process of being salvaged. On the right is a new bluestone works, while in the distance is the repurposed Mexican gypsum mill covered in a veneer of white gypsum powder. (Robert C. Dockery Collection, NSRM.)

An expanded morning Virginia Express steams along the Carson River around 1906. The train has passed the Morgan Mill and is headed toward the Brunswick dam and the spur to the huge mill. The single-track main line has no tie plates and little formal ballast. Closely spaced ties, a profusion of rail braces on the curves, and relatively low track speeds helped keep the railroad running for 80 years. (Homer G. Comstock collection.)

The Brunswick dam diverted all but 10–15 inches of the river into the ditch at far right, which powered the Brunswick's water wheel before returning to the river channel. The mill opened in 1864 with eight ore crushing stamps weighing 1,000 pounds each. The V&T's right-of-way is visible behind the left side of the dam and central fish ladder. (Robert C. Dockery Collection, NSRM.)

Carleton E. Watkins provides a remarkable panorama of the Brunswick in late 1876. The V&T main line from Empire City curves in from the left and follows the line of trees in the foreground. From left to right are the white superintendent's residence, the office with 2-6-0s Nos. 20 and 10 above, the main mill building, and several loaded ore cars. (California State Library.)

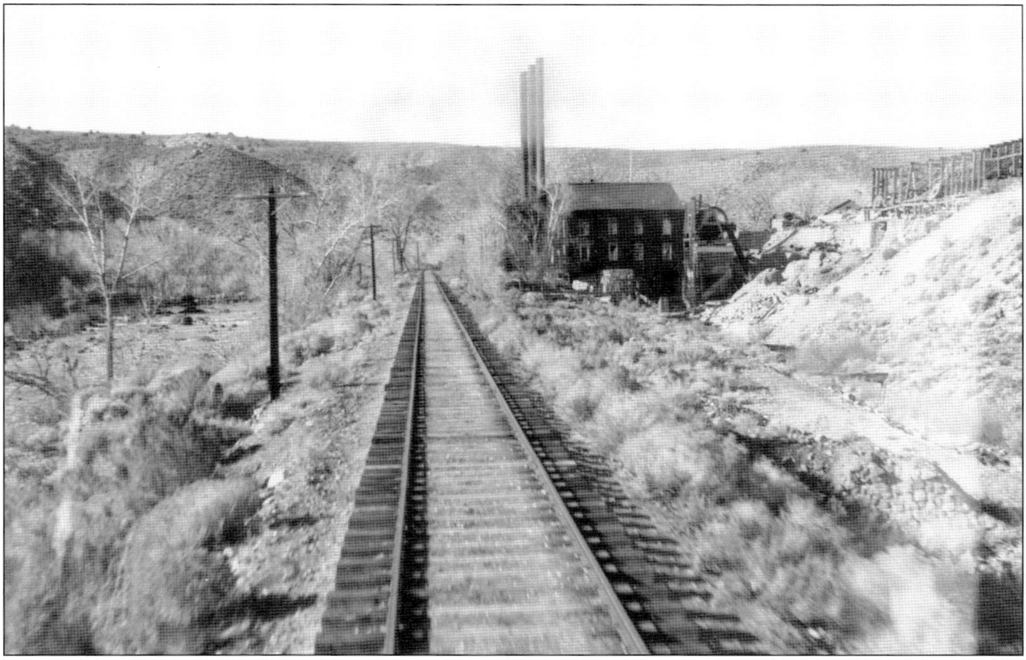

Off-duty Southern Pacific engineer David J. Welch snapped this image through the end window of the coach aboard the train to Mound House in November 1916. All that remained of the Brunswick Mill was the added trackside powerhouse and an exposed rock crusher. At far right are the trestle bents of the V&T's curved 2,156-foot-long spur and 566-foot ore dump siding. The mill last operated in 1910. (Marvin T. Maynard collection.)

Here, in a detail from Carleton Watkins's mammoth view, the V&T main line curves in the foreground past a raised passenger and freight platform for the Merrimac Mill in late 1876. A spur track heads across the ditch and into the main mill building. The low elevation of the battery floor meant the mill could only accept side-dumping cars instead of the V&T's usual bottom-dumping cars. (Robert C. Dockery Collection, NSRM.)

The V&T's spur track comes in on the white rock fill on the right and then proceeds into the main Merrimac Mill building. The mill opened in 1862 with 16 stamps weighing 750 pounds. The V&T's last ore to the Merrimac was from the Chollar Mine in February 1877. Across the river from the mill was a substantial stone quarry. Just downstream was another large cordwood yard.

The small Vivian Mill was on the opposite side of the river. The V&T main line is in the distance at right. The original ore slide was soon replaced by an ore car on a cable incline. Incoming ore was manually pushed in small cars on a bridge across the river and then atop trestlework into the mill. The V&T's last ore deliveries were in January 1893. (Daniel D. Webster collection.)

The Santiago Mill was on a tree-lined site that was popular for picnicking. Cordwood from the V&T was sent down a chute while ore was let down in a three-foot gauge tramway. Built in 1861 as a 24-stamp mill, the Santiago became an asset of the Bank of California in January 1869. The V&T's last ore deliveries were from the Kentuck Mine in August 1893. (Mackay School of Mines.)

One of the largest mills on the Carson River, the Eureka Mill was built in 1861 about one mile below the Santiago Mill and three miles above Dayton. V&T ore cars were let out onto a long trestle where the ore was dumped. An initial 350-foot-long ore chute was upgraded in the 1880s to two counter-balanced incline railway cars that emptied ore into the bin below. (Robert C. Dockery Collection, NSRM.)

The Eureka Mill dam in the distance of this Lawrence & Houseworth stereo view is 125 feet wide. Water power for the mill's 52-inch diameter water wheel was delivered by the 1.12-mile-long flume, which had 30-inch gauge rails on much of it. Two men act as brakemen as two loaded four-ton cars are allowed to roll down to the mill. Mules pulled the empty ore cars back to the ore loading bin.

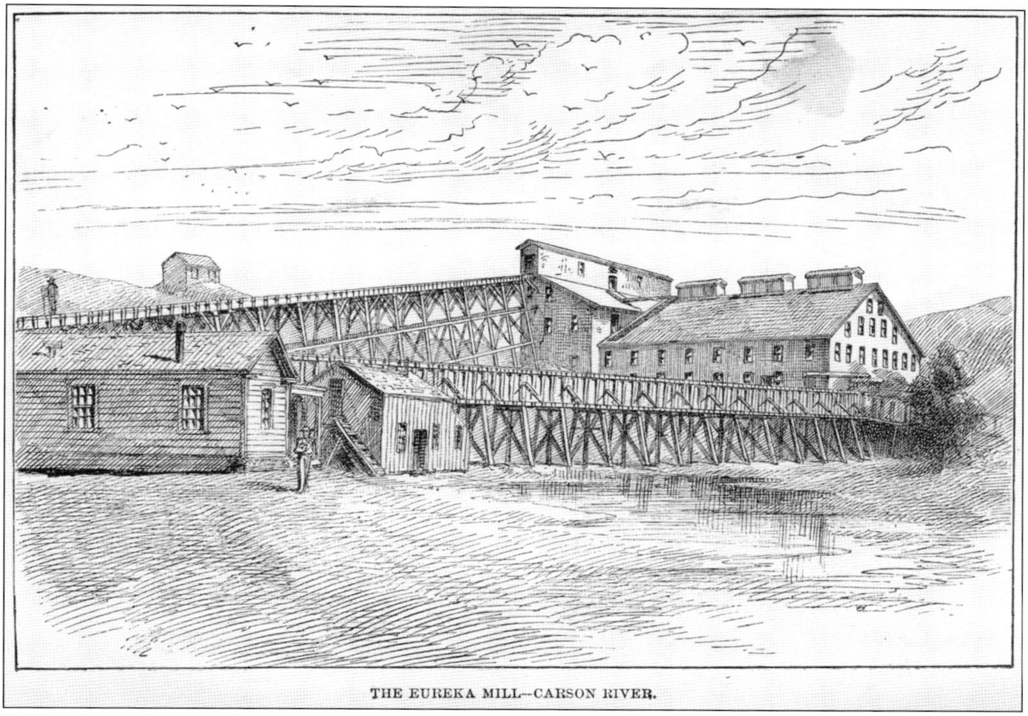

Drawn from photographs, this illustration of the Eureka Mill appeared in Dan DeQuille's 1876 *History of the Big Bonanza: A Full Exposition of the Production of Pure Silver.* Repeatedly rebuilt and enlarged, the mill burned to the ground on May 2, 1892. At the time, the Eureka was crushing 250 tons of ore per day assayed at $20.10 per ton for the Consolidated California & Virginia Mine in Virginia City.

The V&T began delivering ore to the new 12-pan Eureka Cyanide Mill in July 1897. As other mills prepared to shut down, the railroad carried tailings and slimes from the Mexican, Morgan, and Brunswick Mills back to the Eureka through 1901. In disrepair, the mill was sold locally to Herman Davis in 1905. The V&T's Eureka ore trestle was taken down in May 1907. (Special Collections, University of Nevada–Reno Library.)

In 1887, the Eureka Mill Railroad upgraded from a horse to horsepower with a 30-inch gauge 0-4-0 tank engine built by H.K. Porter & Company. Locomotive No. 1 *Eureka* was shipped on a flatcar to Mound House and then by wagon to the mill. The V&T shops built a removable snow plow for the locomotive in 1887 and did repairs on the engine in 1899 and 1901. (Nevada Historical Society.)

Despite its small size, the locomotive weighed 12,000 pounds and proved too heavy for the aging timbers atop the flume. A dedicated right-of-way including two trestles was soon developed immediately north and alongside the flume running to the mill. The 1887 engine worked well at the mill, prior to the big fire in May 1892. (Photograph by James H. Crockwell.)

The *Eureka* is just outside its small engine house. Alongside are the 10 five-ton ore cars built for the mill in 1887 by the V&T's Carson City Shops. The small engine had 8-by-10-inch cylinders and 23-inch diameter drivers. Two flatcars rounded out the rolling stock roster. (Nevada Historical Society.)

In 1900, the Mackay School of Mines senior class visited the Eureka Mill and posed on the train. The locomotive and 10 ore cars were soon sold to the Utah Construction Company for use in dam construction. Apparently discarded, the 0-4-0 was discovered at the bottom of Butt Lake when it was drained in 1996. The engine is now preserved in nearby Chester, California. (Special Collections, University of Nevada–Reno Library.)

A double-headed special train pulls its six loaded passenger cars up the grade out of the Carson River Canyon on June 5, 1938, just south of Mound House. On the point is the V&T's 1872 4-4-0 No. 11 *Reno* and 1913 4-6-0 No. 27—both products of the Baldwin Locomotive Works. The occasion was a railfan excursion chartered by the California-Nevada Railroad Historical Society. (Photograph by William A. Pennington.)

Locomotive No. 11, two excursion flatcars, and coach No. 12 have just cleared Highway 50 on July 17, 1938, and are headed south for the Carson River Canyon. The lone truck has stopped for the train although there are no crossing gates, lights, or bells in 1938. At far left, the V&T main line heads north through Mound House, halfway to Virginia City. (Photograph by Ted G. Wurm.)

Five

Mound House

Halfway House

Situated in Lyon County, Mound House was the location of the halfway house on the 1860s toll road between Carson City and the Comstock. Tolls on the early road ranged from 3¢ per animal to 50¢ for a loaded wagon. The Mound House was named for the natural mounds of gypsite in the area.

With the arrival of the V&T in 1869, Mound House became the halfway point on the initial 21-mile single-track main line between Carson City and Virginia City. Early Mound House was the station point for shipping goods to nearby Dayton, Sutro, and the reduction mills along the east end of the Carson River.

In 1880, the V&T-affiliated Carson & Colorado Railroad began construction on its 300-mile narrow-gauge line from Mound House southeast into southern Nevada and eastern California. The C&C passed into control of Southern Pacific in 1900, just months prior to new ore discoveries at Tonopah and Goldfield. Mound House was a busy transfer point until 1905, when SP bypassed the V&T and built tracks between Hazen and Churchill for its own direct connection to the C&C line. At the same time, SP converted the trackage north of Tonopah from narrow to standard gauge. The V&T serviced the Pacific Portland Cement Company's large plaster works at Mound House until it closed down in 1924. SP abandoned its tracks into Mound House in 1934, and the V&T suspended service four years later. The V&T's rails were finally removed in 1941.

Mound House today consists of residences for several thousand inhabitants plus four legal brothels.

Climbing north from Mound House, the V&T passed through Silver Switch, Haywards, the American Flat tunnel, and Scales, on the way to Gold Hill and Virginia City. It was an uphill climb all the way.

Over the cab of the locomotive *Reno*, photographer Ted G. Wurm looks north through a deserted Mound House in June 1938. A huge gypsum pit was out of sight at far left. On the right side of the tracks were the passenger and freight depots as well as the C&C—later Southern Pacific—tracks to Dayton, Churchill, Tonopah, and points south. (Hart W. Corbett collection.)

Looking northwest at the Mound House passenger depot, the V&T's Virginia City Express of Oxford cars Nos. 13 and 14, smoker No. 3, and coach No. 18 have just pulled in amidst light snow during the fall of 1902. The narrow-gauge C&C track is on the right side of the depot while the crossover V&T track in the foreground leads to an elevated coal transfer dock. (Arthur D. Haig Collection, CSRM.)

Looking south through Mound House, the joint V&T–SP freight depot is on the left in mid-1938. On the right, two women wearing hats walk across the tracks toward the small tool and hand car house. The narrow freight station was custom built in 1881 to fit between the standard and narrow-gauge tracks of the V&T and C&C, respectively. (Photograph by John Debo Galloway.)

Locomotive No. 11 pulls a special train north through Mound House on July 17, 1938, for excursionists of the Railway & Locomotive Historical Society's Pacific Coast chapter. In the foreground is the V&T's 55-foot Armstrong turntable, which was purchased secondhand in 1904. The turntable survives as part of an old bridge across the Carson River. (Photograph by Ted G. Wurm, Hart W. Corbett collection.)

Above, C&C locomotive No. 3 *Colorado* prepares to pull out of Mound House with a 14-car mixed train of both freight and passenger cars around 1888. Visible behind the train are the roof clearstories of the V&T's daily northbound Virginia City Express, which made close connections with the C&C at Mound House. Below, The V&T train has pulled out and a hand car with four men occupies the V&T main line near the towering A.H. Southwick turbine windmill and rectangular wood-frame V&T water car below. The highly mineral groundwater at Mound House was not potable and the V&T routinely brought out fresh water from Carson City. (Both photographs by James H. Crockwell, Special Collections, University of Nevada–Reno Library.)

The narrow-gauge C&C was built by principals of the V&T. The two railroads were both headquartered at Carson City. For the C&C's first 20 years, Henry Marvin Yerington was president of the C&C as well as vice president and general superintendent of the V&T. His only daughter, Jennie Avery Yerington, sits on the pilot deck of the locomotive *Churchill* around 1889. (Yerington family collection.)

Southern Pacific standard-gauge 10-wheeler No. 2156 and the crew of Train No. 190 have brought along their own water car to Mound House. At left is the freight depot shared by the V&T and SP railroads. The freight depot was 134 feet long and a narrow 13 feet, 4 inches wide. (Arthur D. Haig Collection, CSRM.)

While referred to early on as a chalk deposit, both quality rock gypsum and gypsite were mined at Mound House. The first commercial gypsum shipments over the V&T were in December 1877 to San Francisco. Gypsum was used for plaster and in concrete and fertilizer. In the early 1900s, there were at least three gypsum operations around Mound House. Demand for gypsum increased significantly after the 1906 earthquake and fire in San Francisco. The above view looks up at the quarry in 1916 and the aerial tramway down to the plaster mill. Below, small rail ore cars and mules were being used in 1919 to transport excavated rock within the pit. Gypsum mining and a small mill still operate in the unincorporated community. (Both, Roy Mitchell collection.)

Former Nevada governor Jewett W. Adams developed the Mound House gypsum deposit in the early 1900s and marketed the product as "Empire" plaster. He became part of a consortium that founded the Nevada Gypsum Company in 1907, which built a new mill and tramway in north Mound House. The mine and mill were sold in 1912 to the Pacific Portland Cement Company. The sacked product was shipped out in loaded boxcars and sold under the labels Golden Gate Cement and Empire Plaster. In 1922, Portland Cement began building a new company plaster town called Empire, five miles south of Gerlach in Washoe County. The Mound House mill and tram were dismantled by September 1924. (Above, Roy Mitchell collection; below, Robert C. Dockery Collection, NSRM.)

Passenger trains stopped long enough for travelers to imbibe at L.T. McLain's popular saloon across the tracks from the Mound House depot. For 15 years, McLain advertised "Fancy drinks, concocted in the highest style of the art, by one of the best Mixologists in the State." The V&T owned many of the early houses of Mound House and most of them fronted on the V&T tracks. The "white house" at the north end of the yard was one of the more distinctive homes. Below, by 1906, the "white house" had received several additions but its proximity to the tracks remained unchanged. (Above, photograph by Carleton E. Watkins, CSRM; below, photograph by Herman Davis, Nevada Historical Society.)

Roy Mitchell was the chief electrician at the Pacific Portland Cement Company's quarry, tramway, and mill at north Mound House from 1916 to 1924. Portland Cement had a string of company houses at the mill, which employees called "the row." Mitchell's home is identified above as "our house." Below, Roy Mitchell's wife, Mary M. Mauck, and their son Roy Leslie Mitchell pose on the front porch in 1919. The bright yellow passenger cars of the V&T made a daily stop at Mound House, usually delivering only two to three passengers. Cement company employees nicknamed the yellow train "the Banana Special." (Both, Roy Mitchell collection.)

Three miles above Mound House, a spring-fed water tank served the V&T's two dozen steam locomotives in 1876. Another half mile up the track at an elevation of 5,475 feet was Silver Switch with a telegraph station, turntable, and passenger platform above Silver City. Mixed train conductor Judson J. "Jerry" Bray poses on the end platform of V&T Combine No. 16 in March 1889. (Ellen Williams.)

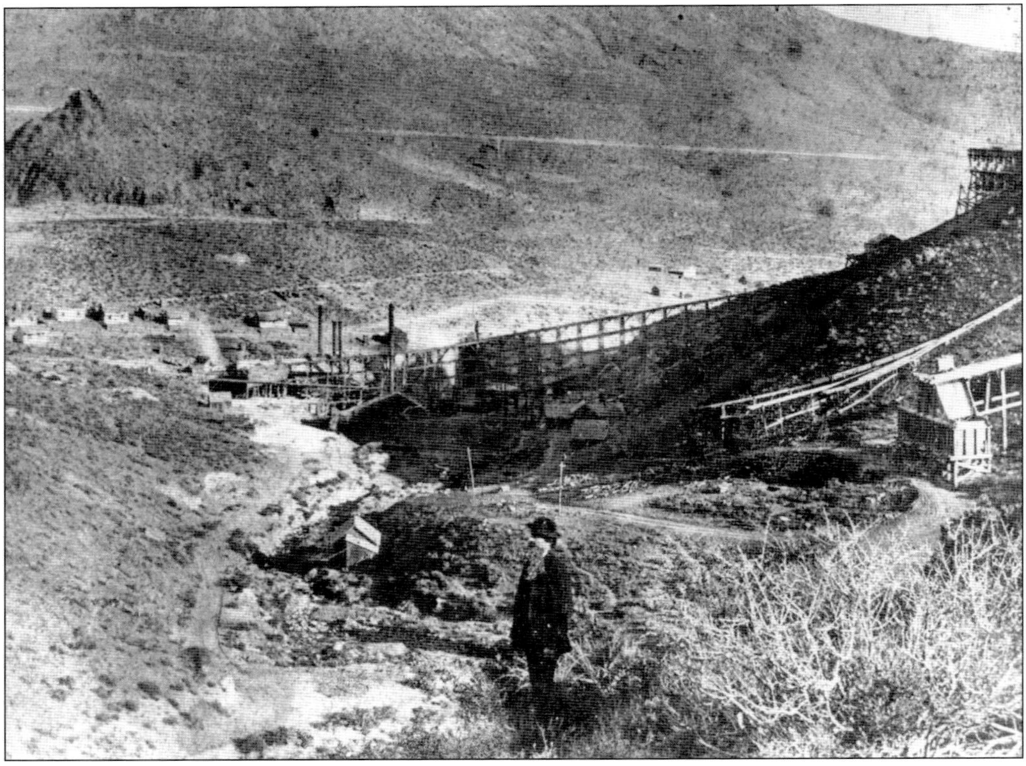

At the end of the V&T's 1.4-mile Silver City track were chutes for delivering cordwood and tramways for transporting carloads of ore to three Silver City mills—the Bacon, Trench, and Kelsey. Loaded freight cars were let down from Silver Switch to Silver City by gravity and then the empties were retrieved by a V&T switch engine. The Silver City Branch was active from March 1870 to May 1880. (Thomas B. Smith collection.)

This panorama from above Devils Gate looks south through Silver City in the 1890s. The V&T's spur track terminated on trestle-work at upper right, on the hillside high above the town during the 1870s. Silver City did not have major mines during the Big Bonanza, but it was home to several of the area's early steam-powered quartz reduction mills. (Photograph by William E. Cann.)

Haywards was a half mile above Silver Switch. The 874-foot-long passing siding was listed on employee timetables as early as 1876 for use by opposing trains. Visible on the left or east side of the main line is one of the V&T's small waiting rooms or passenger shelters. The Haywards shelter was an 8-by-12-foot platform with board-and-batten sides and a shingle roof. (Robert C. Dockery collection.)

One mile above Haywards, locomotives Nos. 11 and 27 prepare to storm through the 568-foot-long American Flat tunnel. Crouched on the running board, photographer "Jerry" Best said he got "roasted" by the engine heat inside the tunnel. V&T engineer John Bartholomew became a local hero when he successfully ran the locomotive *Reno* and its four-car train through a flaming tunnel fire in October 1872. (Photograph by Gerald M. Best.)

Reno photographer "Walt" Mulcahy moved his lighting set-up four times to successfully take this remarkable time exposure inside the dark, abandoned American Flat tunnel. After lying dormant for 67 years, the tunnel was reengineered, stabilized, completely rebuilt, and finally reopened in August 2008 for use by the reconstructed V&T Railroad. (Photograph by Walter W. Mulcahy.)

The V&T secured tracings of the Central Pacific Railroad's snow shed drawings in March 1878, before building 327 feet of its own snow shed a mile east of the American Flat tunnel. Above, the locomotive *Reno* whistles as it exists the shed and approaches Scales with two cars in tow. The shed and snow fences were effective tools against drifting snow, but there were never enough in all of the needed places. Below, during an 18-day snowstorm in January and February 1890, the V&T's snowplow locomotive No. 18, pushed by engines Nos. 20, 14, and 24 with coach No. 4, was attacking heavy snow accumulation at Scales when a snow slide pushed the lead *Dayton* and trailing *Tahoe* off the track. It was a memorable winter. (Above, photograph by Ted G. Wurm, Hart W. Corbett collection; below, Yerington family collection.)

V&T fireman Grover Cleveland Russell poses on June 4, 1938, by locomotive No. 11, which has briefly stopped in front of the water tank and section foreman's house at Scales on American Flat. Scales was so named in the 1870s because of the Fairbanks track scales that weighed loaded ore cars on their way to the quartz reduction mills. (Photograph by Ted G. Wurm, Hart W. Corbett collection.)

The distant mill of the United Comstock Mines Company was a fixture on American Flat for more than seven decades. Built from 1920 to 1922, the operation was the last major new industry on the V&T, but low silver prices forced it to close within five years of opening. The last remnants of the huge mill were deemed a public safety hazard and were demolished in 2014. (Robert C. Dockery Collection, NSRM.)

Six

Gold Hill

Where It All Began

Gold Hill has its origins in 1859 along with Virginia City. The real "gold" was actually in the silver. Surface gold was the earliest discovery, while the Comstock's true bonanza—silver—took significant digging, which was best accomplished by organized mining companies.

The town of Gold Hill was incorporated in 1862 and its heyday extended through the end of the Big Bonanza ore in 1878, when the town population was about 8,000. The Comstock Lode's mining companies, with deep shafts and hard-rock miners, extended from the Rock Island mine on American Flat up through Gold Hill and Virginia City, and to the Utah claim on the north end.

Through the ingenious work of civil engineer Isaac E. James, the V&T wound its main line north from lower Gold Hill, along the west side of the town, through three tunnels, and then on into Virginia City. In Gold Hill, V&T spur tracks delivered building lumber, mining machinery, and a never-ending supply of cordwood fuel for all of the principal ore producers. But only a few of the mines struck paying ore in quantities worth shipping out via the V&T; in Gold Hill, these mines were the Belcher, Caledonia, Confidence, Crown Point, Imperial, Justice, Kentuck, Overman, Segregated Belcher, Trojan, and the Yellow Jacket. Of these, the largest producers were the Belcher, Crown Point, and Yellow Jacket; together, through 1919, they extracted 3.3 million tons of ore, which produced more than $88 million.

The V&T's first train from Carson City arrived at Gold Hill on November 12, 1869. The last special passenger train to Gold Hill was on Tuesday, July 19, 1938. The rails were removed during the fall of 1941 and the deserted mining town was left without rail service. After an absence of 50 years, the steel rails of the revived V&T extended from Virginia City to the historic Gold Hill depot beginning on June 5, 1991. Once again, Gold Hill has its railroad.

Gold Hill developed on the side of a hill and was nicknamed "Slippery Gulch" by the local *Territorial Enterprise*. Mines, bars, businesses, residences, and churches existed side by side. Steep Main Street headed north in the early 1880s toward the imposing Consolidated Imperial Mine at the top of the hill. The V&T's Gold Hill depot was one of the few flat spots in town.

In the transition from American Flat into lower Gold Hill, the Baltimore was one of the substantial mines in 1876. Begun in 1862, it expanded to a three-compartment shaft and was active for 25 years. During that time, assessments totaled $1,015,000, but the production of gold and silver ore was marginal. The V&T main line passes from left to right behind the works. (Photograph by Carleton E. Watkins.)

Just prior to the Gold Hill Cemetery, two miles of spur tracks served the lower Gold Hill mines beginning in the mid-1870s. The V&T spur runs along the tailings ledge to reach the ore bins of the Overman New Shaft. The railroad transported Overman ore to the Vivian Mill through January 1893 and afterward to the Brunswick Mill. As with most mines, stockholder assessments outpaced dividends. (Photograph by Carleton E. Watkins.)

Around 1900, a lone V&T engine pulls two open gondola cars up the grade below the Belcher in lower Gold Hill. Visible far below in the distant right is the cut where the V&T main line entered American Flat on the climb to the Comstock. (Arthur D. Haig Collection, CSRM.)

Two carloads of wood are being unloaded on the siding in front of the Belcher Mine around 1890. The prominent building behind the smokestacks is the superintendents' residence. The derrick structure to the north is an air and drainage shaft. The Belcher was one of the Comstock's largest producers. (Photograph by James H. Crockwell.)

Behind Gold Hill's three-building Central School in the mid-1880s are the V&T's Crown Point spur, the main line with a rock retaining wall, and the imposing main hoisting works of the Belcher Mine. Gold Hill historian Maitland Stanley found that enrollment in 1878 was 1,041 students in the town's four public schools. (Photograph by R.J. Waters.)

The Crown Point, Kentuck, and Yellow Jacket Mines spanned the mouth of Crown Point Ravine. From 1866 to 1869, the three mines were major producers and paid substantial dividends. Above, the Crown Point levied assessments of nearly $3 million and paid dividends of more than $11 million, the last one declared in 1875. The V&T delivered cordwood to the Crown Point via a wood slide on the south approach to the railroad's Crown Point trestle. A lower ore spur on the east side was dubbed "old slippery" by train crews for its steep grade; the track was a proving ground for engineers and the early moguls as crews took turns pulling out long strings of loaded eight-ton ore cars. Below, the Yellow Jacket and its tailings pile spills into town on the north side of Crown Point Ravine. A disastrous underground fire in April 1869 claimed 37 lives. (Above, California Historical Society.)

The 351-foot-long, 85-foot-high Crown Point trestle was the V&T's signature track structure in Gold Hill. Around 1900, the *Genoa* heads the westbound late afternoon express passenger train across the great trestle. In tow is the railroad's winter passenger train of headend baggage-mail-express cars Nos. 13 and 14, smoking car No. 3, and coach No. 18. The speed across the trestle was limited to three miles per hour.

The 1869 construction of the imposing trestle consumed 185,000 board feet of lumber, and two workers lost their lives. In 1879, V&T superintendent Yerington secured bids to replace the bridge with a riveted structure but the projected cost exceeded $10,000. The trestle was routinely painted in a dark red-brown "fireproof" paint. Large cables stabilized the bridge against strong canyon winds and Washoe Zephyrs.

In 1924, 4-6-0 Second No. 25 has just cleared the Crown Point trestle while shoving three open hopper cars destined for the Charles Butters Mill in Virginia City. The Sutro Tunnel Coalition paid the V&T almost $56,000 in 1935 to relocate the main line so the Sutro group could conduct open-pit mining under the trestle. An engineered fill was constructed and V&T crews dismantled the trestle the following summer.

The *Reno* eases into the Gold Hill yard on June 4, 1938. Ahead, from left to right, is flanger No. 51, the combination freight and passenger depot, and a 12-by-19-foot section tool house. The 1872 locomotive brought along an empty boxcar to be loaded with concentrates from Virginia City. (Photograph by Ted G. Wurm, Hart W. Corbett collection.)

The wall calendar is dated 1898 in this remarkable view inside the V&T's Gold Hill depot. Behind the young agent at the public counter are maps of some of the destinations where patrons could purchase tickets to or consign freight along the Vanderbilt Lines, the Burlington Route, or via ocean-going vessels. Also behind the agent is a ticket window into the separate ladies' waiting room. (Nevada Historical Society.)

"The boys" gathered on the platform outside the depot office in 1904 where former telegraph operator Ernest F. Hall was the new station agent. The combination depot consisted of a small freight warehouse that was lengthened, an added office and ladies waiting room on the north end, and a residence for the station agent that was created by filling-in under a platform eave. (Dale B. Darney collection.)

A trapezoidal roof was added atop the office in 1912 to help deflect snow and rainwater on the gradually sinking office end of the depot. On August 22, 1933, boxcar No. 1011 sits on the house track outside the freight warehouse. V&T service to Gold Hill at the time was a small daily motorcar, supplemented by an occasional mixed steam train. (Photograph by David L. Joslyn.)

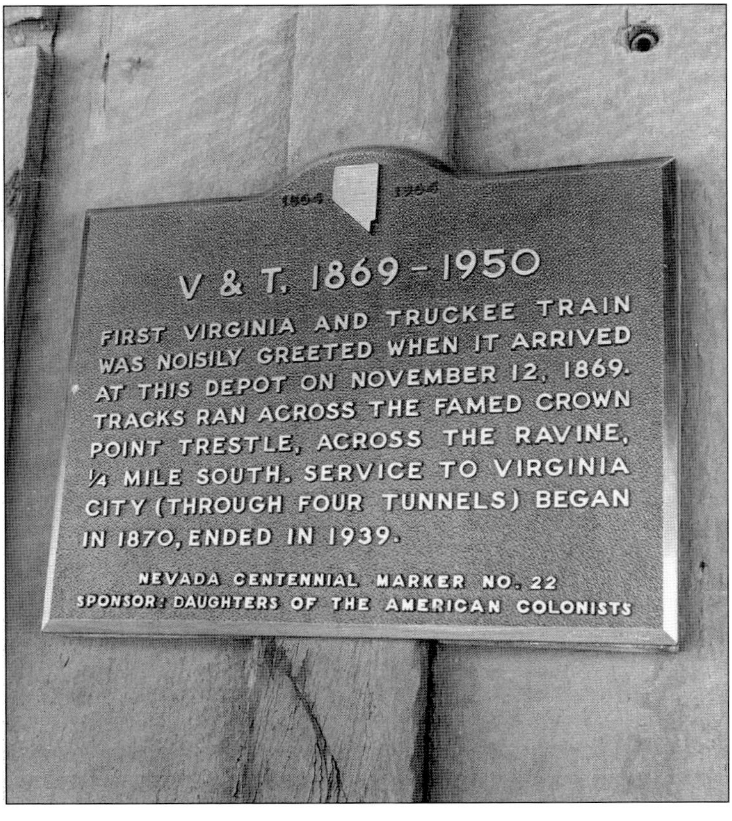

The V&T closed the Gold Hill depot in October 1937 and the building sat unused until it was sold for one silver dollar in October 1946 to Storey County. The Daughters of the American Colonists affixed a plaque to the building during Nevada's 1964 centennial. Now restored, the depot has become a destination for the summer trains of the revived Virginia & Truckee Railroad. (Photograph by Robert H. Austin.)

Heading east out the depot, the V&T mainline negotiated a 19-degree curve—the tightest on the railroad—across Main Street, now Nevada State Route 342. On the northeast corner was the hall of the powerful Gold Hill Miners' Union. Miners organized early on to secure a $4 per day wage for eight hours of underground labor. Local members had several labor confrontations with the V&T and the local sheriff in the 1870s; the union was determined that unemployed miners should have priority on V&T jobs in Storey County. Built in 1870, the wood structure had an imposing false front. The abandoned building finally collapsed in November 1946 under the weight of heavy snow. (Above, photograph by Paul B. Darrell, CSRM; below, Frank L. Slater Jr.)

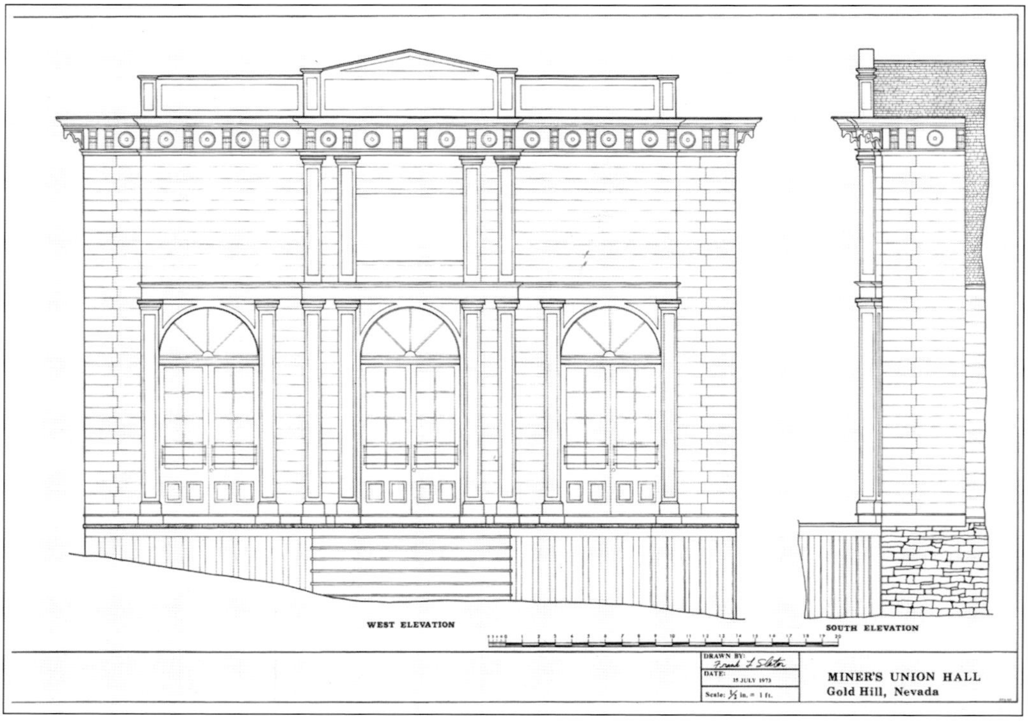

Locomotive No. 27 charges eastward across Main Street as it prepares to pass between the Miners' Union Hall and Liberty Fire House No. 1. In 1937, Gold Hill's Main Street—the southern approach to Virginia City—was still a dirt road. The Comstock's stature as an established tourist magnet was still a year or two away. (Photograph by A. Sheldon Pennoyer.)

Leaving the Gold Hill business district, the V&T plunged into the first of three tunnels between the town and Virginia City. Wood-timbered and sheet metal–lined, the 144-foot-long Homestead tunnel was excavated on a curve and on an ascending grade. The tunnel was repeatedly plagued by settling ground. During the first two years, the final two miles of tracks were operated as part of the Gold Hill yard limits. (Photograph by Ted Steinmetz.)

While in definite decline, Gold Hill still presented an impressive image in 1894 with several blocks of businesses still intact along Main Street. From the Crown Point trestle on the right, the V&T main line made a giant loop past the wood and coal yard and the combination depot on the right, across Main Street, and then into the Homestead tunnel on the lower left. (Photograph by William E. Cann.)

High above the business district, the "Little Gold Hill Mines" were the original Gold Hill claims staked by James Finney, Henry Comstock, "Sandy" Bowers, and others in early 1859. Included were the Empire, Imperial, Challenge, and Bowers Mines. Production of gold and silver ore from 1866 to 1876 totaled more than $15 million.

The V&T's 465-foot-long Yellow Jacket Tunnel was excavated through solid rock. Sparks from passing locomotives constantly plagued the tunnel timber sets and wood portals. The tunnel burned in June 1902 and again in August 1920. Abandoned for nearly 50 years, the tunnel was reopened by the revived V&T in July 1987; it continues in daily use. (Robert C. Dockery Collection, NSRM.)

Outside the east portal of the V&T's Yellow Jacket Tunnel was the east or new Yellow Jacket. The mid-1870s mine was sunk by the Bonanza firm of John W. Mackay, James G. Fair, James C. Flood, and William S. O'Brien as one of the "third line" of vertical shafts. The mine cost $2 million and reached a depth of 3,060 feet. Only barren ground and floods of hot water resulted.

Above, the V&T main line heads right to left, from Gold Hill, past the Ward Mine, and toward the "Divide" and Virginia City. A V&T spur track delivered lumber, machinery, and cordwood to the Ward beginning in the late 1870s; unfortunately, no paying ore resulted. Explored to the 2,600-foot level, the shaft was later used for ventilation and for pumping out water from connecting mines before the buildings and machinery were razed during World War I. Below, the 97-foot-long Ward or Washoe Divide tunnel was the shortest of the V&T's seven formal tunnels. The bore was just east of the old 190-foot-long wagon toll road tunnel, which bridged the Divide between Gold Hill and Virginia City beginning in 1864. (Both, Robert C. Dockery Collection, NSRM.)

Seven

Virginia City
Heart of the Comstock

The Comstock Lode was discovered in 1859 on the future sites of Gold Hill and Virginia City, along the eastern side of 7,870-foot-high Mount Davidson—formerly Sun Mountain. The "first line" of gold and silver mines were surface diggings and shallow shafts extending only several hundred feet below the surface. A "second line" of mining shafts going down 1,000–2,000 feet quickly developed slightly east through the center of town. A "third line" of deep mines reaching 3,000-plus feet followed farther east beginning in the mid-1870s. Well over $300 million was produced during bonanza years in the 1860s and 1870s. The Comstock swelled to its peak of nearly 40,000 inhabitants.

Building east from Gold Hill, the new V&T reached a small yard and platform just beyond the Gould & Curry works on January 29, 1870. The railroad's original approximately 20-by-75-foot first depot still stands at F and Washington Streets in Virginia City.

In mid-1872, the V&T main line was pushed north through the E Street tunnel to reach the Ophir works, which had contributed along with more than a dozen other mines toward the original construction of the road. New freight and passenger depots and a coach shed were also built but succumbed to the Great Virginia City Fire of October 26, 1875. New structures were built in 1876, and of these, only the freight depot survives.

While originally built to serve the freight transportation needs of local mines and mills, the V&T's connection with the transcontinental rails of the Central Pacific at Reno effective October 1, the year 1872 began an additional profitable business handling passengers, mail, and Wells, Fargo & Company Express as well.

After 68 years and declining revenue, train service between Carson City and Virginia City was suspended in mid-1938 and the rails were removed in 1941.

After an absence of nearly 35 years, steel rails were once again laid on the original right-of-way for use by the revived Virginia & Truckee Railroad beginning in July 1976. The new tracks have been in continuous service ever since.

Captured during the Big Bonanza of 1873–1878 in a view toward the Divide, Virginia City became a 24-hour city with miners toiling underground in three eight-hour shifts, seven days a week. Mines, mills, a profusion of drinking establishments, hotels, other businesses, mansions, family residences, schools, churches, and even opera houses co-existed side by side. (Photograph by Carleton E. Watkins.)

The V&T arrived and departed Virginia City via the short Divide or Ward tunnel. In the early 1870s, the main line passed by the developing Julia Mine, the V&T's early car shop, and the first four stalls of the road's Virginia City roundhouse, as seen in this John Calvin Scripture stereo view. In the distance is the "richest city on earth"—both a raucous town and a center for refinement and culture.

The V&T's roundhouse was expanded to eight stalls for up to eight locomotives in October 1876. Loaded ore cars were accumulated around the shops where employees could keep a watchful eye on the precious metals. Up behind the roundhouse are the Hale & Norcross and the Savage Mines. (Photograph by R.J. Waters, Thomas B. Smith collection.)

Arriving in Virginia City, locomotives cut off their train and proceeded to the turntable, where they were turned. Available on the turntable lead were water, sand, wood, and coal for the return trip to Carson City. No. 11 loads up on June 4, 1938, under the watchful eyes of, from left to right, engineer Grover C. Russell, conductor William A. Wise, and fireman Harold F. Brooks on the tender. (Photograph by Ted G. Wurm.)

Due east of the V&T roundhouse was the combination shaft, a "third line" mine representing the combined interests of the Chollar-Potosi, Hale & Norcross, and Savage properties. A 2,280-foot-long V&T spur delivered machinery, lumber, and cordwood. Excavated to a depth of 3,250 feet, it was the Comstock's deepest vertical shaft. But despite $7 million in assessments, the mine never returned a dividend. (Photograph by R.J. Waters.)

The New Nevada Mill was built in 1887 on the Chollar claim in southwest Virginia City. The Nevada was the last Washoe process mill, and the next year, it became the Comstock's first mill to use electric power. The V&T delivered ore to the mill from both the nearby Hale & Norcross and Savage Mines. (Edward R. Strong collection.)

The V&T main line skirted around the east side of the Hale & Norcross Mine. A spur track was connected when ore traffic warranted. The railroad delivered machinery, lumber, and cordwood on the west side of the mine. William Sharon lost control of the H&N to the Bonanza firm of Mackey, Fair, Flood, and O'Brien during a bitter stockholders' fight in 1869. (Mackay School of Mines.)

The V&T's original Virginia City freight and passenger depot was built in 1870 at F and Washington Streets, just past the Gould & Curry's ore bins and in the shadow of the landmark St. Mary's in the Mountains Catholic Church. The restored 20-by-75-foot building now serves as the passenger depot for the revived Virginia & Truckee Railroad in Virginia City.

The 586-foot-long E Street Tunnel was constructed under Taylor Street and directly in front of St. Mary's. The extension allowed the V&T to develop a new yard, passenger station, freight depot, and train shed up on E Street and to reach the Ophir Mine toward the north end of Virginia City. The rails were removed in 1941, and several studies have looked at re-excavating the old tunnel.

An all-coach train of at least six cars confirms that this is a special train about to depart the passenger depot on E Street in Virginia City. Sunday excursion trains had special fares and were very popular on the V&T. They were also very lucrative for the railroad.

The long shadows indicate that locomotive No. 11 is about ready for its late afternoon departure from Virginia City around 1907. The 4-4-0 has reassembled the four cars so that the two mail-express-baggage cars are immediately behind the engine, followed by the gentlemen's smoking car and a trailing coach. The passengers are already on board, and the US mail is the last item to be loaded prior to departure.

The traveling Virginia City baseball team poses in front of the V&T's new coal-burning locomotive before departing from the E Street passenger station. Engine Second No. 25 was received by the V&T in March 1905. But within three years of its arrival, the new 4-6-0 was converted to burn fuel oil due to the high cost of coal.

The 31-by-98-foot passenger station was built in 1876 on the former site of the freight depot, which burned in the Great Virginia City Fire of 1875. From left to right, the board and batten structure contained a waiting room, ticket and telegraph offices, directors' board room and walk-in vault, and a baggage room. Closed in May 1938, the building was razed in August 1945. (William A. Pennington collection.)

On the opposite side of E Street from the V&T were the Consolidated Virginia Mine assay office. Controlled by the Bonanza firm of Mackey, Fair, Flood, and O'Brien, the Consolidated Virginia was the largest precious metal producer on the Comstock, with more than $42 million paid in dividends through 1880. (Photograph by Carleton E. Watkins, Mackay School of Mines.)

Immediately north of the passenger station was the V&T's second car shed, where the four-car passenger train was serviced and sheltered from sunshine and winter snow during its daily midday layover in Virginia City. The 224-foot-long board and batten shed was built in 1876. In 1912, the building's paint scheme was changed from light yellow to more utilitarian dark red with white trim. (Ted G. Wurm collection.)

The winter of 1900–1901 was underway when the photographer looked south through the E Street yard. The date is confirmed by the air brake hose and Sams link and pin couplers on the empty cordwood flatcars alongside the Consolidated Virginia Mine and the profusion of old steam equipment on the flatcar following the celebrated first use of electricity on the Comstock in October 1900. (Thomas B. Smith collection.)

The approximately 30-by-125-foot freight depot was built at the northwest corner of E Street and Sutton Avenue in 1876, on the former site of the Central Silver Mining Company's mill in Virginia City. The office and public counter were on the south end of the large freight warehouse. The building was recently purchased by Storey County. (Frank L. Slater Jr. collection.)

Hundreds of sacks of potatoes fill the raised end platform of the freight depot around 1900. Potatoes were an obvious staple on Comstock menus. The smokestacks behind the depot belong to the Consolidated Virginia Mine across the street. (Photograph by William E. Cann, Nevada Historical Society.)

V&T locomotive Second No. 25 prepares to depart the freight depot on May 3, 1938. During the 1930s, No. 25, mail & express No. 21, and combine No. 15 were the equipment most likely to be pressed into service when there was a freight car for Gold Hill or Virginia City. The published schedule gave the train a three-hour midday layover before returning to Carson City. (Photograph by Roy D. Graves.)

The north end of the freight depot had a variety of uses. The area was the Virginia Lumber Yard of Oliver Lonkey and E.R. Smith during the late 19th century, the Standard Oil Company's auxiliary bulk oil facility during the 1920s, and the Hobart Estate Company's Virginia City wood yard during the 1930s. (Photograph by Paul B. Darrell, CSRM.)

Looking up E Street, the V&T main line extended north to reach the Ophir and the upper works of the Union Consolidated Mines. Pictured above after a c. 1890 snowfall are, from left to right, the Ophir warehouse, the ore dump, main hoisting engine room, boiler room, central shaft, pump room, machine shop, and blacksmith shop. In the 1870s, the Ophir's boilers consumed up to 23 cords or three flatcar loads of wood per day. Below, two flatcar loads of cordwood are spotted outside the boiler room at the Union mine. (Above, Edward R. Strong collection; below, Mackay School of Mines.)

Behind the string of bottom-dumping eight-ton ore cars on the main line is the V&T's spur track serving the ore bins of the Ophir and the Consolidated Virginia Mines. Above, the Ophir had a Babcock hydraulic elevator that lifted and distributed the ore into bins with hinged chutes for loading seven V&T ore cars at a time. The illustration below was drawn "from photographs taken on the spot, by John S. Noe, and E. Hurd, of Virginia City, Nevada," specifically for Dan DeQuille's 569-page *History of the Big Bonanza*, published in 1876. The switch engine, most likely *J.W. Bowker*, prepares to pull out a string of loaded cars from below the ore bins of the Consolidated Virginia. (Above, Mackay School of Mines.)

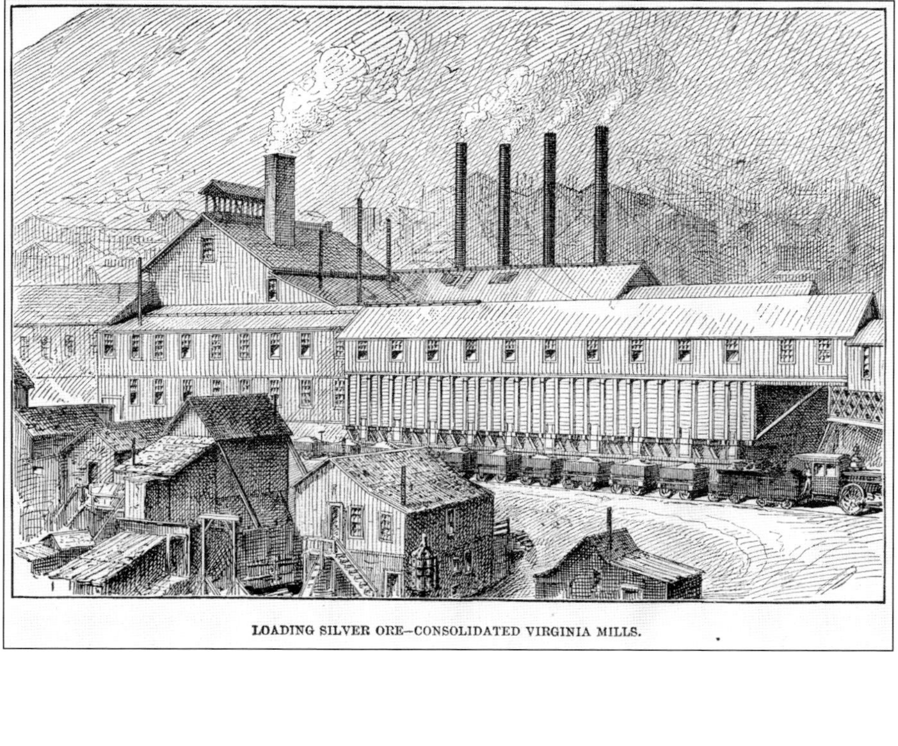

LOADING SILVER ORE—CONSOLIDATED VIRGINIA MILLS.

The V&T's low line was constructed in mid-1876 to serve the new Consolidated California & Virginia, or "C&C," shaft east of the Consolidated Virginia. The line passed through new 391-foot-long L Street tunnel No. 7 along the way. Part of the "third line" of shafts, the C&C was excavated to below 2,500 feet and helped extract the fabulously rich ores of the Big Bonanza.

The stub track north of the C&C was extended by two long stringer trestles to reach the new ore dumps of the Union Consolidated Mine in October 1879. On September 9, 1891, local miscreants kicked loose the brakes and chains on several loaded flatcars, allowing them to crash at speed into four empty flatcars on the Union trestle. While several flatcars were demolished, no one was injured.

A string of empty V&T ore cars is lined up north of the ore dumps at the Union. The Union Consolidated was organized in January 1875 by the Bonanza firm and included underground access to the connecting Mexican and Sierra Nevada Mines. The Union Consolidated shipped ore via the V&T from 1879 to 1884. Unfortunately, the company never paid any dividends. (Michael A. Collins collection.)

The V&T locomotive No. 4 *Virginia* was a popular switch engine in Virginia City during the 1890s. The town's namesake was built in 1869 by the Baldwin Locomotive Works for $16,333. The wood-burning 2-6-0 served the V&T for five decades. It was eventually sold to a San Francisco scrap dealer, where it was cut up in 1919.

Virginia City still looked impressive from the Combination shaft in 1890, but the city was on a gradual decline. Pumping out hot water from the deep mines ceased in 1886. There was a resurgence of mining activity after electricity arrived on the Comstock in 1900, but it never rivaled the glory years of the 1873–1878 Big Bonanza.

Charles Butters's plant was the largest tailing cyanide mill in the United States when it opened in 1902 down in Six-Mille Canyon east of Virginia City. In 1907, the facility was converted to a conventional mill with a crushing capacity for handling ore from Tonopah. An aerial tramway extended from the V&T low line down to the mill until it was torn down in mid-1926 and moved to Elko County.

Nothing affected the V&T schedule like a good snowstorm or a series of storms and the resultant snow blockades, damage to the right-of-way, and inevitable derailments. The winter of 1915–1916 saw many trains delayed and even annulled. In January 1916, snowplow locomotive No. 18 led the charge, backed by two and three engines, to re-open the line into Virginia City. Above, three locomotives and the four-car passenger train work their way toward the E Street tunnel. Below, No. 18 plows its way into the E Street yard opposite the freight depot. It was a memorable winter. (Both, Tom L. Williamson Collection, CSRM.)

In 1929, the V&T's daily passenger train was changed from running between Reno and Virginia City to operating from Reno to Minden and return. V&T gasoline motorcars Nos. 23 and 99 were pressed into service from 1929 to 1938 to handle much of the passenger traffic to the Comstock. The No. 23 *Canary's* much-celebrated first trip to Virginia City was on July 23, 1917, with a carload of local dignitaries.

Locomotive No. 11 is manually turned on the 60-foot-long Virginia City turntable in June 1938. The Virginia City roundhouse was reduced to only four stalls, and all of the engines were gone. Virginia City was equally deserted. It was the last year that the V&T ran trains between Carson City and Virginia City, ending 68 years of service to the Comstock. (Photograph by Ted G. Wurm.)

Eight

MINDEN

FERTILE CARSON VALLEY

With an infusion of cash from a temporary increase in business during the early 20th-century Tonopah boom, the V&T looked to expand its territory. The railroad had done preliminary surveys for extensions south from Carson City to Genoa and also Wellington in the late 1870s. V&T vice president Henry Yerington was receptive when the H.F. Dangberg Land & Live Stock Company approached the railroad with the offer of a right-of-way to the new Dangberg town of Minden one mile north of Gardnerville. The branch would extend 15.2 miles south from Carson City and serve the developing agricultural, dairy, and livestock traffic in the Carson Valley.

A new V&T Railway Company was incorporated on June 24, 1905, to succeed the old V&T Railroad. Ground was broken in April 1906, and the branch line opened on July 4, 1906.

From the railroad's Stewart Street spur in south Carson City, the new branch meandered due south past the old Carson & Tahoe Lumber & Fluming Company wood yards, the Indian boarding school at Stewart, the Nevada State Prison Farm, across the Carson River, to Hot Springs, Douglas, the stockyards, and on into Minden in Douglas County. The grade was gentle, the curvature was minimal, and the costs were held down by using relayed rails. The only freight and passenger depot was at Minden.

The new branch became a popular destination for Sunday picnic excursions from Carson City. Blocks of stock cars transported sheep and cattle brought in and out for fattening up prior to slaughter. Carloads of petroleum products, agricultural vehicles and implements, and even a carload of new automobiles became fairly routine. In 1929, the route of the V&T's daily mixed passenger and freight train was changed from Reno–Carson City–Virginia City to Reno–Carson City–Minden.

The V&T brought in freight right up to the end. The last scheduled train from Minden was on May 31, 1950, ending 45 years of service to the Dangberg family's new town and the rich agricultural valley south of Carson City.

Locomotive No. 26 heads south down Stewart Street in November 1949, pulling mail and baggage No. 23 and combine No. 18. On the left is the Nevada Lumber Company, operating on the site of the old Carson Box Factory and later the wood yard of the Sierra Nevada Wood & Lumber Company. The shiny tank in the distance marks Standard Oil's local bulk distribution facility. (Photograph by Ted G. Wurm.)

The Carson Indian School was operated by the federal government with students from the Navajo, Paiute, Shoshone, and Washoe tribes. Founded in 1890, it was moved in 1905 to Stewart, three miles south of Carson City. The community was named for Nevada's longtime US senator William Morris Stewart. The school was closed by the US Bureau of Indian Affairs in 1980.

Locomotives Nos. 11 and 27 pause with an excursion train alongside the raised wooden platform and 10-by-20-foot passenger shelter at Stewart on September 21, 1941. The occasion was the Comstock Express operated for 150 passengers, members of the California-Nevada Railroad Historical Society. The wood-frame shelter burned down in May 1949. (Photograph by Dick Jenevein.)

With the two passenger cars cut off and parked, locomotive No. 26 shoves a tank car load of fuel oil onto the 990-foot-long spur track to the boiler shop on the grounds of the Indian school. Now owned by the State of Nevada, the historic facility is being converted to a museum and cultural center. (Photograph by Ted G. Wurm.)

Locomotive No. 27, the V&T's last steam locomotive to be purchased new, poses on the trestle over the Carson River six miles south of Carson City. The occasion was the May 29, 1949, Farewell Excursion of the California-Nevada Railroad Historical—the organization's fourth and final trip over the V&T since 1938. Peering out the cab is engineer William Recker, who was a 35-year veteran of the V&T.

The six-stringer, four-pile trestle over the Carson River was 480.6 feet in overall length. The original structure washed out in the flood of March 1907, and a Southern Pacific pile driver was brought in to rebuild it and the SP's Carson River crossing at Dayton. After suffering repeated fires, the track speed was restricted to five miles per hour. (Photograph by John Stiles.)

Hot Springs was eight miles south of Carson City at the base of 5,951-foot Hot Springs Mountain, just over the Douglas County line. Among many natural hot spring mineral pools in the area, the most famous was David and Harriet Walley's Hot Springs, built in 1862 on the nearby emigrant trail below Genoa. The original 11-room resort and ballroom burned in 1935.

Three miles north of Minden, Douglas housed the V&T's section crew facilities for the Minden Branch. The morning south-bound train headed by 4-6-0 No. 26 steams toward the 1905 Douglas bunkhouse and privy, well-shaded by cottonwood trees of the same vintage. The wood-frame structures were closed in March 1945 and sold locally the following year. (Photograph by Charles M. Clegg Jr., CSRM.)

A mixed train headed by locomotive No. 17 *Columbus* pulls into Minden in 1906. Boxcar No. 1013, right, served as the temporary station and telegraph office until the 32-by-60-foot freight depot was completed in September 1906. The first station agent, Herbert H. Coffin, lived in the nearby tent. (Walter S. Young collection.)

The wives of V&T vice president Henry Yerington and financier Ogden Mills—son of V&T President Darius Ogden Mills—alight from the railway's new 70-foot-long McKeen Motor Car No. 22 at the Minden depot during an inspection trip on July 5, 1910. Clara Viola Bender Yerington, left, hosted Ruth Livingston Mills, who joined her husband for the trip out from New York. (Yerington family collection.)

Half a dozen boxcars occupy the west leg of the V&T wye at Minden in March 1911. From left to right are the Meyer's Mercantile Company farm machinery warehouse, the four-story Minden Flour Mill and silos, and Meyer's general merchandise store, which opened in May 1907. In 1911, the town's population was 100. (Yerington family collection.)

A variety of horse-drawn vehicles make pick-ups and deliveries along the west side of the depot. When the Dangberg family's plans fell through for a nearby hotel, the V&T added the separate 16-by-28-foot passenger waiting room in early 1909 along the south end of the depot. (Special Collections, University of Nevada–Reno Library.)

Beginning in September 1929, the six-day-a-week Reno-Minden steam train alternated service with the V&T's McKeen motorcar. The schedule gave the crew a four-hour layover at Minden to accomplish unloading, car switching, and reassembling of the consist for the afternoon return to Carson City and Reno. At midday in August 1933, the cars are parked near the depot. (Photograph by David L. Joslyn.)

Around 1931, V&T mail & baggage No. 13 and express No. 14 are parked at midday just west of the depot for easy vehicular access. A truck from the nearby Minden Butter Manufacturing Company is backed up to the express car, where reusable crates of butter are consigned with the onboard clerk of the Railway Express Agency. (Vernon J. Sappers collection.)

Behind the plow and underneath the accumulated snow is V&T locomotive No. 18 *Dayton* at Minden during the winter of 1937–1938. The 4-4-0 was an 1873 product of the Central Pacific Railroad Shops in Sacramento. At an elevation of 4,709 feet, Minden averages nine snow days per year. The record month was January 1916, when snowfall totaled 52 inches.

Pulling into Minden on May 3, 1949, on the main line at the right, No. 26 has backed its train up to the depot on the siding alongside the station. The 1907 station agent's house is at far right. During the preceding year, the V&T handled 430 inbound and 71 outbound carloads of freight at Minden. The local population was only 400. (Photograph by Robert M. Hanft.)

Locomotive No. 27 had the honor of pulling the V&T's last scheduled train out of Minden on May 31, 1950. The entire town came out for the departure ceremony, which included a shotgun salute and "Taps" played by a lone bugle. Minden had struggled to retain the V&T, and there was not a dry eye when the last train finally departed. (Photograph by Alfred M. Rose Jr.)

To supplement train service and compete with increasing rubber-tired vehicles, the V&T invested in buses and trucks. In January 1929, its Virginia-Truckee Transit Company was incorporated to carry passengers, parcels, Railway Express, and US Mail between Reno, Virginia City, Carson City, Gardnerville, Yerington, and Lake Tahoe. V-T bus No. 21 stops outside the post office at Gardnerville. V-T Transit outlasted the railway by more than 20 years. (Photograph by Norman W. Holmes.)

V&T locomotive No. 29, a 1916 Baldwin 2-8-0, was named for the late Robert C. Gray, who brought the V&T back to life in Virginia City beginning in July 1976. His son, V&T president and general manager Thomas H. Gray, continues his father's vision. The State of Nevada has built an additional 12 miles of track between Gold Hill and Carson City. Steam trains run from May to October.

The largest and finest collection of preserved locomotives and rolling stock of the Virginia & Truckee is held by the Nevada State Railroad Museum at Carson City. Among the restored gems are the 1875 locomotive No. 22 *Inyo*, 4-6-0 Second No. 25, and 1910 McKeen Motor Car No. 22—all of which have been impeccably restored and periodically operate at the museum. It is a must-see when visiting Carson City.